# LIGHT OVER LUNDY

# LIGHT
## OVER
# LUNDY

*A history of the Old Light
and the Fog Signal Station*

Dr Myrtle Ternstrom

Whittles Publishing

*Published by*
**Whittles Publishing**,
Dunbeath Mains Cottages,
Dunbeath,
Caithness, KW6 6EY,
Scotland, UK
www.whittlespublishing.com

ISBN 978-1904445-29-6

*Typeset by* Samantha Barden
*Printed by* Bell & Bain Ltd., Glasgow

*In fondest memory of Peter and Barbara Cole*

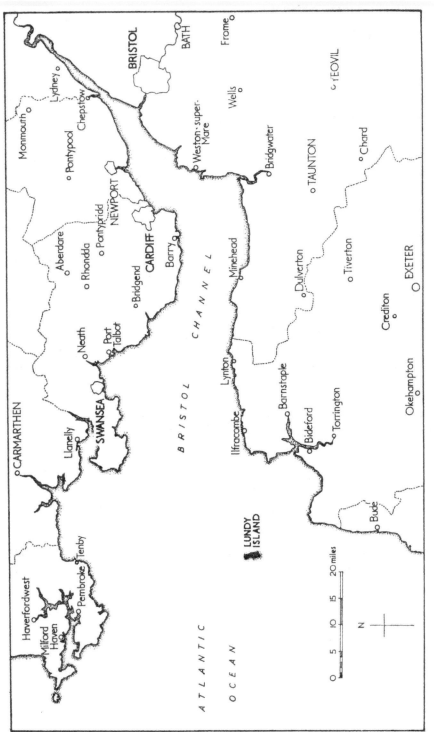

Map of the Bristol Channel

# Contents

# Acknowledgments

I am most grateful to Trinity House for access to and permission to use the legal archives, the records deposited at the Guildhall Library, Corporation of London, and the Engineers' archives. I am particularly appreciative of the kind help received from the staff of the Engineers' Archive at the Isle of Wight in obtaining copies of maps, plans and drawings.

I also wish to thank the following friends for their help and interest in this book:

- Members of the Heaven family for access to their family papers;
- Walter Cooke and John Hinshelwood for correspondence and photographs concerning the repairs to the Old Light;
- Tony Cutler for reading and discussing the MS, and for help with maps and plans;
- The late John Dyke for permission to copy a drawing from *North Devon Heritage* No. 4;
- Jeff Evans for copies of newspaper cuttings;
- Mrs Valerie Fenwick MA FSA MIFA for permission to use the print of the *Iona*;
- Keith Gardner for permission to use the photoprint of Serres' painting;
- Rosemary Hague for permission to use material from Hague and Christie, 1975;
- Diana Keast for access to the Harman papers;
- The Mission to Seafarers for permission to quote from the diary of the Revd Ashley; to Stan and Joan Rendell, who drew this to my attention, and to Miss R. Charles who made the transcription from the MS;
- The *North Devon Journal* for permission to quote extracts;
- Peter Rothwell for help with illustrations;
- R. Derek Sach for the gift of his collection of photographs;
- And especially to my editor, Dr Elaine Rowan, for her work in preparing the manuscript for publication.

# DEFINITIONS

*AK* Assistant Keeper

*Argand Lamp* The use of a cylindrical wick within a glass chimney that allows a current of air through the centre of the burner, and enables more efficient combustion of the fuel. A further refinement of this was a device for force-feeding the oil, which allowed the light to burn for longer before the wick had to be replaced. The wicks could also be placed one inside the other to give a brighter light. As the lamp produced heat, ventilation was necessary.

*Catadioptric Light* The beam is concentrated more intensely by the use of both reflecting and refracting optical apparatus.

*Catoptric Light* The rays of light are reflected from behind the source by mirrors, which increase the strength of the beam.

*Dioptric Light* The light rays are refracted by the use of glass lenses in front of the light source. The lenses, designed by Fresnel, consisted of a small spherical central lens, around which concentric serrated rings were ground out of solid glass in steps, or concentric zones, by which the beam was refracted into parallel rays concentrated in the required direction. The weight and density of the lens was considerably reduced by Fresnel's design (the annular or polyzonal lens).

*First Order Apparatus* The entire lantern apparatus is usually of 14 ft width (4.26 m). The beam has a focal distance of 3ft 0.25 ins (920 mm). According to Findlay (1890), a first order lenticular apparatus "is one of the most beautiful objects in the world…nearly twelve feet high and six feet in diameter, constructed with the utmost skill and refinement, and involving in its structure some of the highest principles of applied science".

*Flotsam* Floating wreckage

*Frames* In order to provide a revolving light, the lenses were mounted on a frame which was turned around the fixed light. In the case of a light of the first order the frame was octagonal in order to carry eight lenses. The apparatus was rotated by a clockwork mechanism with a system of weights.

*Holophotal Light* The addition of glass zones above and below the central lenses, from where the light is reflected back to the source, which augments the strength of the beam. Thus all the light from the source is utilised in one direction.

*Jetsam* Jettisoned goods

*Parabolic Reflector* A curved polished metal reflector placed behind the light source.

*PK* Principal Keeper

*Zones* A set of crystal lenses mounted so that they send the light in one parallel direction.

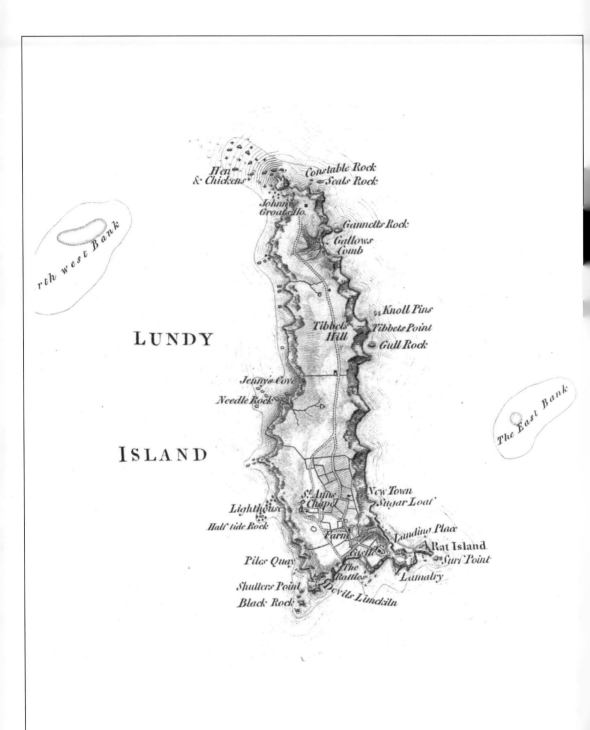

Lundy Island, reproduced from the 1820 Ordnance Survey map
(with the kind permission of the Ordnance Survey)

# Introduction

L undy is a granite plateau with an elevation of some 400 ft (122 m), with an area of shale in the southeast of the island where the weathering of the rock has carved a bay and beach that provide a landing place. From there a steep road climbs and curves to the top of the island.

Archaeologically, the island is of considerable interest. Finds of flint tools and the remains of Bronze Age huts show that it has been inhabited from the earliest times. Four Romano-British inscribed stones and a considerable contemporary burial complex are found in the burial ground, close by the Old Light, together with the remains of a medieval chapel. Elsewhere on the island are traces of medieval longhouses and settlements, and the archaeological sequence continues to the granite quarries of the Victorian industrial age.

Apart from a period of forty years during the reign of Henry III, when the king found it expedient to keep the island in his own guardianship to prevent rebellion and piracy, Lundy has been an estate in private hands. It passed from father to son or, more often, from owner to buyer, until it was bought for the National Trust in 1969. Until the nineteenth century Lundy remained little known and little visited. It was difficult to get there and it could be even more difficult to leave. There was very little to attract the visitor, unless drawn by simple curiosity or in search of the seabirds which, with the rabbits, provided the main part of the islanders' income. Much of the island is of moorland character with (usually) a good supply of water. There are areas of pasture, with some arable for keep, so that sheep have been farmed through most of the island's history — the flock in recent years has numbered about 600.

Lundy was left much to its own devices and, probably because of its remote insignificance, was free of taxes and tithes. It could be argued this was fair, since the island received no services or support from the mainland authorities. Trinity House was the first national body to have any establishment on the island, and this brought the first sector of the population that was not dependent on the owner, as well as increased contact with the outside world. Trinity House was later followed by the Lundy Granite Company, Lloyds for signalling, the GPO for post and telegraph, the Board of Trade for rocket life-saving apparatus and Admiralty coastguards. Another important change during the 19th century was that the Heaven family made Lundy their permanent home, the only owners known to have done so during all its history.

As the 19th century saw the end of Lundy's isolation, the century that followed has reflected rapid national economic and social change, and par-ticularly advances in communications. These have culminated in the withdrawal of all the public bodies from the island (with the exception of Trinity House), and the end of Lundy's ambiguous legal standing. The island now has status as a Site of Special Scientific Interest, and is the country's first National Statutory Marine Reserve. It has been extensively supported by the Landmark Trust, a charity that administers Lundy by lease from the National Trust, and by project funding from outside bodies. It is now accessible for many more people to enjoy its scenery, its wildlife, climbing, diving or bird watching, and to experience the island — its peace and its beauty.

# Chapter 1

## THE BEGINNINGS OF LUNDY LIGHTHOUSE: 1610–1821

The *Nautical Description of the Coast of Britain* published in 1812 described Lundy Island as (THGLA 1812):

> "Lofty, and encompassed with high craggy Cliffs, which are Inaccessible almost in every Part, except at a Sloping Declivity of the Cliff near the S.E. End of the Isle, where a boat can land with offshore Winds. Lundy is about 2½ Miles in length from NW to SE and about two thirds of a Mile in Breadth, and is readily distinguish'd; and can be seen at 8 or 9 Leagues distance with tolerable clear Weather. Lundy is not only useful in pointing out the Entrance of the Bristol Channel, but its Roadstead is also of great Utility; as it affords shelter with Westerly Winds, to the Pilot Skiffs, from Bristol and Ilfracombe, which are often waiting here for Arrival of Ships; and on their being seen from this Island…the Pilots go off to them…the distance from Lundy to Kingroad [Bristol] is about 88 miles…The Entrance of Bristol Channel is on either side of Lundy Isle, but ships, or vessels of any kind, coming from the southward with Southerly Winds, ought to prefer the Passage between the South End of Lundy and Hartland, to the Passage between the North End of the Isle and Wormshead."

The island represented at once both a haven and a hazard to mariners. It offered shelter and an anchorage from westerly gales, but presented a steep rocky coastline that was unlit, and was from time to time obscured by fog. Although the island is only three miles long and less than one mile wide, its rocky coastline measures some twenty miles around, and there is a large tidal variation of eight metres (26.2 ft). Lundy also has strong tide races at the north and south ends, and sudden changes of wind direction to the east or north could make even the normally sheltered east side roadstead hazardous. Bristol was a significant trading port, and Lundy's position at the mouth of the Channel was important to vessels setting out or returning from ocean voyages as well as to the local coasting traffic. One estimate was that there were as many as one million ships passing Lundy in a year. There are records of up to 300 ships in sight at one time, and as many as 170 anchored in the bay.

With the rapid growth in the volume of shipping in the later eighteenth and nineteenth centuries there was inevitably an increased number of shipwrecks, then running at about two a day, and a Select Committee was set up in 1836 to investigate the causes. It was reported that apart from those caused by the natural hazards of fog and violent weather, others had been brought about by low levels of seamanship and navigational skills, inadequate charts, a want of harbours of refuge, the defective construction of ships, or the drunkenness of crews. It seems certain that there were more wrecks than have been recorded.

Apart from the paucity of communications, wrecks were a rich source for the theft of goods for which the evidence would most probably have been suppressed. Customs officers were frequently at a distance and poorly paid, therefore lenient or corruptible. There was no lifesaving organisation. The administration of wrecks was an uncertain area of the law until the Act of 1852, by which Receivers of Wreck were appointed.

The provision of lighthouses could do little to remedy these problems, but they could give warning of hazardous rocks and coastlines, and provide a beacon for purposes of navigation. Many lighthouses had been privately operated by individuals who had been granted patents by the Crown, and standards were haphazard. But by 1785 the efficiency of the lights had come under criticism, and Trinity House became more closely concerned with their operation. As the patent grants expired, they began to take over full responsibility.

When Thomas Benson, a North Devon ship owner and merchant, acquired the lease of Lundy from Earl Gower in 1750, he was well aware of the advantages that could accrue to shipping, to the island, and to himself with the erection of a lighthouse there. He petitioned Trinity House that it would help to avert "...misfortunes happening to many Ships, Lives, and Valuable Merchandize, which have been Annually lost there". Benson did not support his petition with any figures giving the number or nature of the shipwrecks, and three counter-petitions against the idea were advanced by the merchants and traders of the North Devon ports. They would have preferred a site at Hartland Point, and the Trinity House brethren at Bristol were concerned about the burden of lighthouse tolls on trade, so Benson's petition failed. Apart from the *Daniel*, "lost uppon Londay" (THGLA 1751) sometime between 1610 and 1620, Lundy wrecks are not recorded before 1757, but fifteen ships were reported lost on or near the island's coasts before there was a fresh initiative to set up a lighthouse.

A certain Captain Rogers, of Cornwall, put forward a plan for a lighthouse which, he considered, in appearance and effect, would be totally different from every light in England. It is not clear if this was the same plan adopted by the Merchants of Bristol, whose trading activities were at a peak in the eighteenth century, but an anonymous visitor to Lundy wrote (North Devon Record Office 1787) that his party

> "...took a walk to the Chapple and the Beacon Hill, to examine which was the highest spot in order to erect a Light House, the Merchants of Bristol having offered to build one at their expence if Mr Cleveland would give them Liberty, and had appointed to give him the meeting that week on the Island to fix a proper spot, on examining the ground, we thought the Beacon Hill the highest and most proper spot for the Purpose."

The name of Beacon Hill suggests that there may have been a warning or signal beacon there, for which there remains no evidence.

A letter patent was obtained by Trinity House to license the collection of lighthouse tolls for Lundy, but still no lighthouse appeared, possibly because either the money was not available or the owner (John Cleveland) objected. He sold the island in 1802 and the new owner, Sir Vere Hunt, was certainly very keen to have the lighthouse. He wrote to Trinity House to urge the matter forward, and was informed (THGLA 1803) that

> "...if the Merchants, Owners, and Masters of ships concern'd in the Trade navigating past the Isle of Lundy will present an application address'd to this Corporation... requesting that a light may be established on that Island for the safe Guidance of navigation, and signifying their consent to pay an adequate Toll or Duty for its Maintenance such application will be taken into immediate consideration."

Another sixteen years passed before the necessary signatures and subscriptions were submitted on behalf of ship owners, merchants, and ships' captains. Finally it was decided that a lighthouse on Lundy would be of the greatest help to ships in entering the Bristol Channel. The danger of wreck on dark nights or in foggy weather could be avoided and the loss of vessels and men would be reduced. By that time Sir Vere Hunt had died and been succeeded by his son, who was approached for the lease of the chosen plot of land.

Lundy was not only the scene of wrecks, but a most convenient centre for prolific smuggling. This was rife in the late eighteenth and early nineteenth centuries following the imposition of heavy taxes on tea, brandy and other items, to pay for the wars with the French. Around 1721 a Richard Score or Scores rented Lundy at a time when it was neglected by its owners. He used it for storing smuggled goods, which were eventually seized by the Customs authorities. In 1723 the crew of the customs vessel avoided the possibility of their being spotted before arrival by rowing to the island, where they seized a large quantity of tobacco and spirits. Scores was soon followed by a William Cuthbert, who was running brandy in and out of Lundy, and who had three judgements passed against him in 1727. He managed to evade arrest and the authorities could not pursue their prosecution against him.

Benson himself was caught in 1750 for the evasion of duties on large quantities of tobacco that he had shipped to Lundy. He was fined £8,300 — a huge sum at that time, and one that is indicative of the scale of his transactions. By the nature of the clandestine operations involved, we have records only of such operators as were caught, but when the master of the *Nottage* was fined and examined in 1762 he gave the impression that the island was a general exchange for all kinds of contraband. In 1785 the Cardiff Collector was driven

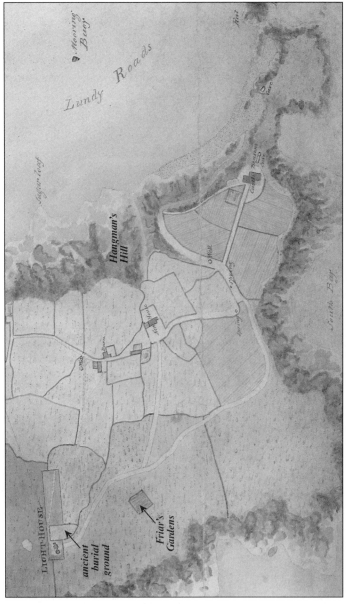

The lighthouse was placed on the highest point of the island, on the west side. 'New House' is the current Old House (from a section of Trinity House map No. 1319 1820)

to comment "…there never lived yet a man on the island of Lundy who was not connected with smuggling" (Smith 1989).

The coasting vessels and the pilots were heavily engaged in the trading of smuggled goods along the channel ports. The commander of HMS *Beaver* was despatched from Appledore to Lundy in 1783 in an effort to catch them. A large Polperro lugger, the *Swallow*, was anchored in the bay, becalmed, but immediately the naval man-of-war was sighted the crew cut their anchor and began rowing away with their long-sweep oars. The captain and crew, who had gone ashore, were left to follow in their boat as best they could. The next morning the crew of the *Swallow* saw the *Beaver* not far behind them, towed along by her crew rowing in their small boats. A race ensued, which only ended towards the evening when, three miles from the mainland, the *Beaver* dropped her anchor, her crew rowed on unimpeded, boarded the *Swallow*, and took her back to Lundy. In her hold they found huge quantities of tea, brandy, and gin. Such were the profits to be made, that it is highly probable that the arrests affected by the customs were only the tip of the iceberg of the trade run on Lundy (National Archives 1783).

Between Benson's original proposal in 1750 and the construction of the lighthouse, there were records of a number of ships lost on or near Lundy. However, the details that have survived are more useful for forming an idea of the nature of the trade of Channel shipping rather than providing an accurate figure of the number of wrecks. Bristol at that time was a busy port, and the Bristol Channel one of the most important trading seaways. The North Devon coast and the Channel were also referred to as the sailor's grave.

The *Marie*, loaded with coal, was stranded and a total loss on 19th September 1757, followed by the *Susanna* on 4th September 1768 which was found abandoned to the north of the island, "painted red and yellow" (Larn and Larn 1995). The *Jane* was a brigantine out of Kinsale, carrying coal from Swansea to Dublin. The master put ashore at Lundy on 12th July 1792 to save the crew, and some of the cargo was also salvaged (doubtless to the advantage of the islanders, for whom fuel was always a problem). In the following year on 19th February 1793 the *Nancy and Betty* sank near the island with the loss of all crew. This was followed by the *Polly Bray* of Padstow, lost near Lundy with all hands, and then the *Wye*, a Chepstow ship which ran ashore on Lundy in December 1796, a total loss in which all the crew perished.

A wreck occurred on a date variously given as 27th January or 20th February 1797, which has bequeathed its name to the bay on the western side: Jenny's Cove. The *Jenny*, a 78-ton three-masted schooner, was carrying a cargo from Africa to Bristol which included gold dust in leather bags and elephant tusks. The ship also mounted "eight old and very bad two-pounders for which we had scarce any shot, two swivels, some wall pieces and twelve muskets".

The ship struck the rocks and sank, and the only survivor of the four or five passengers and the crew of thirty was the chief officer, who was later sent back to Lundy to carry out salvage. He managed to lift only some of the ivory (Langham 1994).

---

### Loss of the *Jenny*

We state with extreme concern the loss of the ship *Jenny*, Captain Buckle of Bristol, on his return from the coast of Africa, with a valuable cargo of ivory, dye-wood, gold dust, and other merchandise. Having for some days experienced very foggy weather, the ship's reckoning could not be accurately kept, and in consequence she unfortunately ran ashore on Lundy Island, when the ship went to pieces, and the captain and the crew, except the Mate, unhappily perished.

(The Times 1797)

---

The first wreck of the new century was the *Myrtle Tree, en route* from the Baltic to Dublin. She was stranded and a total loss on 14th January 1800. On the 2nd July 1804 the *Western Flying Post* (1804) reported the arrival at Ilfracombe of

"…a most beautiful lugger, *Fanny* of Fowey, captured in a calm with 400 ankers [about 3000 gallons] of spirits on board, off the Isle of Lundy a few days since by the *Nimrod* cutter…She had run 600 tubs on shore at Lundy previous to capture."

The next wreck to have been recorded is the *Baltic*, 8th February 1809, which set out from Cardiff for Lundy, but foundered before she reached the island although the crew was saved. Equally fortunate was the crew of the *Concord,* bound for London from Bristol, which sank near Lundy on 20th November 1810 and was lost.

There were six further wrecks before the Lundy lighthouse was put into commission. The *Estrella de Mar,* a schooner under Spanish sail out of St Ubes for Bristol, was stranded near the present Battery in 1811, a total loss, although the crew survived. At the end of the year a brig was de-masted off the south end. Three or four men were seen to be sitting on the stern, who were saved when the *Britannia* took them in tow to Ilfracombe, though the mate had gone over with the mast and was drowned. The owner of the island, Vere Hunt, was pleased to witness the fortunate rescue, although he lost the chance to go ashore in the *Britannia* for which he had waited during three bitterly cold and stormy weeks.

Five years later the sloop *Rover* was wrecked on the Knoll Pins on the east side of the island on 17th November 1816, when carrying coal from Newport to London. An unidentified ship foundered, a total loss, in February 1819 and six of the crew lost their lives, though the rest were saved. This was followed on the 1st May by the *Unity*, a sloop bound for Barry from Charlestown which foundered north of Lundy, though her crew was rescued. The last was the *Lamb,* a schooner lost in a gale off Lundy on 20th January 1820. Nothing at all was seen of the ship, but three dead bodies and an oar marked 'Lamb' were washed up in the small bay north of the present Battery. It was afterwards called Lamb Cove, although that name did not survive for long.

In March of 1819 subscriptions were received from merchants, ship owners and masters of ships from Bristol, Swansea, Chepstow, Gloucester, Bideford, Barnstaple, Minehead, Cardiff, Newport, Ilfracombe and Pembroke ("very numerously and respectably received") and orders were at last given to proceed. In May of 1819, Captains Lorne and Gooch were sent to Lundy by Trinity House to select the site for the lighthouse. They chose Beacon Hill, and recommended that the height of the tower should be 80 ft. An agreement was reached with De Vere Hunt that he would be paid £500 in return for a 999-year lease of two acres of land at a peppercorn rent, and the right for Trinity House to quarry stone "...in great Plenty and proper and fit for the Building" (THGLA 1819). Daniel Alexander, the Trinity House consultant engineer, sent one of his men to survey the island and compile a map, and was asked to submit plans for the lighthouse. The lighthouse as it is seen today is instantly recognisable in these beautiful drawings. The discerning eye will detect that changes were made later in the structure of the lantern.

### Navigation of the Bristol Channel

LUNDY ISLAND LIGHTS — Notice has been given, that in compliance with the request of a numerous body of Merchants, Owners, and Masters of Ships, interested in the navigation of the Bristol Channel, the Corporation of the Trinity Board have directed a Light House Tower to be erected on the Island of Lundy, wherein 2 distinct Lights, an Upper and a Lower Light, will be exhibited for the benefit of Navigation. The Uppermost Light will revolve in a horizontal row, without any interval of darkness, illuminating the whole circle of the horizon: -The Lower Light, placed 30 feet below the upper, will shew a fixed and steady light, extending over 90 degrees of the horizon only, or from N.N.W. to W.S.W. by compass; by which arrangement all vessels entering the Bristol Channel will be enabled readily to distinguish the lights on the Island of Lundy from all others in that vicinity. The necessary works for the exhibition of the aforesaid Lights are proceeding with all possible dispatch, and are expected to be completed in about two months.

FLATHOLM LIGHT — With a view to the farther security of Vessels navigating the Bristol Channel arrangements have been made for the Improvement of the light on the Island of Flatholm, by exhibiting a revolving Light with Argand Lamps and Reflectors in lieu of the present Coal Fire, and preparations are now making for effecting this desirable object in the ensuing spring.

(Taunton Courier 1820)

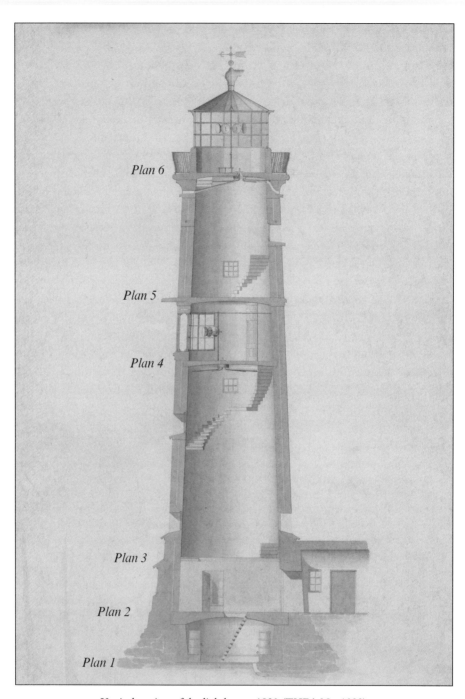

Vertical section of the lighthouse, 1820 (THEA No. 1322)

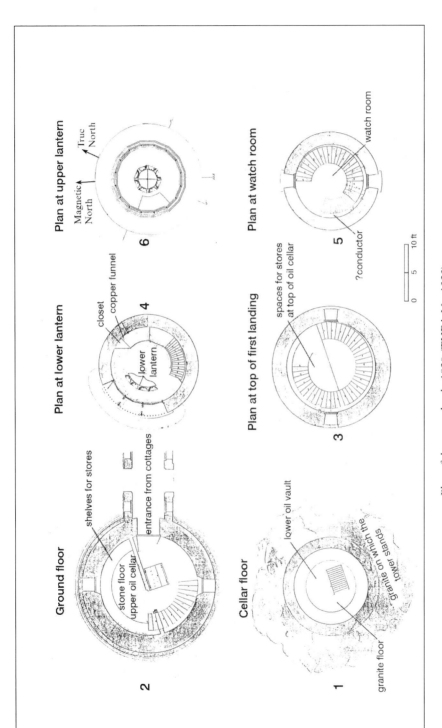

Plan at upper lantern

Magnetic North

True North

6

Plan at lower lantern

closet
copper funnel

lower lantern

4

Ground floor

shelves for stores

entrance from cottages

stone floor
upper oil cellar

2

Plan at watch room

watch room

?conductor

5

Plan at top of first landing

spaces for stores
at top of oil cellar

3

Cellar floor

lower oil vault

granite on which the
granite floor        tower stands

1

0    5    10 ft

Plan of the tower levels, 1820 (THEA No. 1323)

The effectiveness of a lighthouse illumination was later summarised as being determined by the source of light, the apparatus used to focus the beam in the required direction, the adaptation of the beam and the optical apparatus to each other, and the distinction between one light and another, as well as the altitude and position of the lighthouse itself. These criteria were made, as in the nature of a developing science, with the benefit of hindsight. In 1820 Lundy lighthouse was placed proudly atop the highest point of the island.

The lighthouse was built between 1819 and 1820 by Joseph Nelson, and the lantern was constructed by a firm under the direction of a Mr George Robinson. The tower is magnificently built of island granite and, as Alexander had little involvement after the completion of his design, the credit for the building of it belongs to Nelson and his superintendent of works, James Turnbull. It has been remarked: "Vitally important as the actual design of the tower is, its construction calls for a high degree of skill and administrative abilities, coupled with very great courage, patience and physical endurance" (Hague and Christie 1975). The circular tower is exceptional in having a cavity construction with double granite walls 0.07 m (3 in) apart, and is the highest in Britain, with the lantern 164.5 m (540 ft) above the high water mark. The gable end of the dwelling faces into the prevailing westerly winds and is supported by two sturdy columns, which has been described as a "gesture of defiant confidence" (*Ibid*).

The granite tower of the lighthouse was 29 metres high (95 ft), and the cost of the building, including the keepers' quarters, was £10,276 19s 11d (the equivalent of around £620,000 today). Accounts for other various expenditures to the end of 1820 show that Trinity House had spent in the region of £13,000. They were empowered to charge tolls of one farthing per ton for UK vessels (except for ships in royal service) passing the lighthouse, collected at the ports of arrival and departure. Foreign vessels were charged at double the rate. The principal ports employed Trinity House Collectors, who took payment for inward lights before the ship could be registered at Customs, and for outward lights before the ships' papers were cleared for setting sail.

The dues were high, and from 1818 to 1820 gave Trinity House a huge profit. Trinity House defended this, maintaining that the profits were used to relieve poverty among seafarers and their families by providing pensions, almshouses and reliefs. In 1821 the tolls for Lundy provided revenue of some £1054 against outgoings of £1164, but the expenses for that year included payment for some of the setting-up costs, and in subsequent years the profit was very considerable. The net profit between 1822 and 1828 was £3,074. By 1840, it had risen to £1,132. There was also an income for the island owner from haulage and minor repair work, extra trade for the farm, and some income from the accommodation of workmen sent by Trinity House.

The Trinity House agent at Bideford, Thomas Grant, notified the Elder Brethren that the lighthouse was put into service for the first time on 21st April 1820. There were two lights. The upper, consisting of eight lamps, was mounted in the lantern, and by means of a remarkable newly-developed revolving mechanism (THGLA 1820) gave

> "a quick flashing white light, which was an innovation in lighthouse optics... [although] the light revolved so quickly that no period of darkness was detectable between the flashes so in effect this appeared as a fixed light".

The Argand burner employed a circular wick with a central draught of air within a glass chimney, providing a bright, steady flame. It showed brightly for five seconds before being obscured for twenty seconds. The beam was intensified and directed by the use of parabolic reflectors made of copper. The revolving light reflectors were fixed to the sides of a frame which was turned by means of a clockwork mechanism and the length of the flash was controlled by the speed of the revolution. There was a stove in the lantern room, as sperm oil would not flow well in a cold atmosphere. Ventilation was provided by a pipe through the roof, which emerged below the weathercock. In some cases keepers also used the stove to warm their food, although this earned them a reproof as it caused adverse effects to the lantern atmosphere.

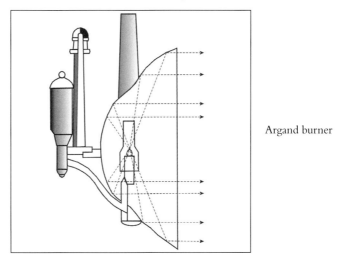

Argand burner

The lower light, having four lamps, was mounted 9.14 m (30 ft) below the upper light to show a fixed white light over 90° NNW to WSW, although it was found that at a distance of five miles or more the two lights merged into one. Sperm oil was used for the lights at the rate of about 2728 litres (600 gallons) per year, for which the annual cost was £177 8s 2d (the equivalent of nearly £11,000 today). However, the price of oil fluctuated: between 1823 and 1833 the lowest price was 3s 3d per gallon and the highest 6s 3d.

The keeper's duty was to light the lamp at sunset and to keep it burning in good order until sunrise. The tower was painted white as it also acted as a daymark; in the early part of the nineteenth century navigation was not an exact science, and daymarks are still useful for small craft even now. In studying the changing names of places on Lundy, it is interesting to note that the only ones to have survived from the early maps are those of coastal features used as navigational markers. That there was a need for improvements to navigation is shown by Lloyds' registration of 50,000 wrecks between 1854 and 1879, and their estimate that there was one shipwreck every day around the British Isles. Even this figure is most probably a considerable underestimate, since not all wrecks were reported. A wreck that was within reach was a valuable commodity indeed, and there are many descriptions of their proceeds leading to disputes, theft, fighting, and even murder.

### Instructions to lightkeepers

1. You are to light the lamps every evening at sun-setting, and keep them constantly burning bright and clear, till sun-rising.

2. You are to watch by turns, half the night each; one till 12 o'clock, the other the remainder; he who has the first watch one night is to have the second watch the night following, and the light is by no means to be left without one of you attending it. The keeper who has the first watch is to call the other, and leave the lamps fresh trimmed and burning bright.

3. You are to be careful that the lamps, reflectors and lanterns, are constantly kept clean and in order; and particularly to be cautious that no lamps, coal or candles be left burning any where, so as to endanger fire.

4. In order to maintain the greatest degree of light during the night, the wicks are to be trimmed every three hours, taking particular care that they are exactly even on top.

5. You are to be careful that the reflectors are properly cleaned every morning, keeping them free from scratches or other damage, and using only the polishing powder and leathers provided.

6. You are to see that none of the oil, stores, goods, or materials be wasted, embezzled, or stolen; and to observe economy and good management, in every respect, yet so as always to maintain a perfect good light.

7. If any of the lamps, reflectors or windows are broken, or other damage be done to the lighthouses, through carelessness or negligence of the light-keepers, the repair thereof is to be paid for by the person through whose carelessness or negligence the damage occurred.

8. You are to keep an exact account of the quantity of oil received from time to time, the number of quarts, pints, half pints and gills consumed each night, and deliver the same to the agent every month, together with an account of the quantity remaining in store.

9.  You are not to admit any person whatsoever into the lighthouse, nor suffer any damage or obstruction which may occasion the least interruption of light to navigation.

10. Any light-keeper being drunk, or neglecting any part of his duty, will be subject to dismission, or forfeiture of such part of his wages as the corporation shall judge proper.

11. No light-keeper will be permitted to appoint another person to watch for him, except in cases of sickness or unavoidable necessity, not even then unless the person so appointed shall be approved by the agent, who is to make him such allowance as he shall think reasonable, and to deduct the amount of it from the wages of the light-keeper for whom the duty shall have been done.

12. You are to keep a journal of all occurrences and observations, and to be particular in describing all circumstances attending them, and to communicate the same on the form provided for that purpose, once a quarter, or oftener, if necessary.

13. The most careful attention to and strict observance of all the above regulations will be expected of you; and also that you take care to keep every part of the lighthouse, as well as your own apartment, perfectly clean and in good order; as on any complaint of the want of cleanliness at any time, or at the annual visitation in particular, you will be immediately dismissed.

14. You are to communicate upon all matters relating to the lighthouse and the duty of your office with the agent appointed to superintend the same; and any representation you may at any time have to make upon any occurrences in any way relating thereto you are to deliver verbally or in writing to him, in order to be by him transmitted to the corporation's secretary, to be laid before the Board.

INSTRUCTIONS to be observed by the LIGHT-KEEPERS, in respect of the Girdle, Leather Case and Tin Box provided for their use in Trimming the Lamps:

15. Great breakage of cylinders continually taking place at several light-houses belonging to this corporation, for the prevention of which, and the promotion of cleanliness, the above-mentioned apparatus has been provided; the light-keepers are especially directed to make use thereof at all times, and in the manner following, previously observing to cover the cylinder tongs with leather:

16. The belt is to be strapped round the body.

17. The cylinder, when taken from the lamp for the purpose of snuffing, is to be immediately deposited in the leather case.

18. The snuff, when taken from the wick of the lamp, is to be put in the tin box (in which a little damp sand is to be kept), and the sponge at the opening is intended to cleanse the scissors from the snuff.

19. The cylinder tongs and scissors are to be put on the hooks affixed to the belt as occasion requires.

(National Archives 1829)

A quay was constructed at the Landing Bay on Lundy, with a marker stone which is still in place despite many landslips. It was necessary to have a storehouse near the landing place where supplies were kept until they could be moved up to the lighthouse, and at first this was rented from the proprietor. Carrying supplies up to the lighthouse including coal and heavy cans of oil was a laborious process, especially as at that time there was only the old steep path leading up from the beach to St John's Valley. From there (the present Battlements) Trinity House built a road to the plateau, or rather a track that could accommodate carts. Two donkeys were sent over to relieve Trinity House men of the work of carrying the goods between the store and the road, and Trinity House was charged an extra seven shillings per month each for their grass keep. But the problem of the theft of coals from the store and disputes over the use of the storeroom were less easily resolved, and eventually Trinity House built their own store.

The landing bay and old steep road, from a painting by Dominic Serres in 1775
(courtesy of Keith Gardner)

The Trinity House stone at the landing place
(courtesy of R. Derek Sach)

The quarters for the keepers and their families were equally solid, built with a connecting passage to the tower. The principal keeper was housed on the ground floor, and the assistant above, each having a living room with a large fireplace, coal hole, pantry, and two bedrooms. The privies were separate in the southeast corner of the compound and the water came from an island well some distance away.

In 1821 Trinity House built a small cottage on their land to the east of the lighthouse (now called Stoneycroft) which was for the use of their agent and visitors. With sudden changes of wind direction, or the rising of a gale, sailing ships were unable to depart and there were occasions when visitors could be delayed in their return for several days. Smuggling was rife at that time and the considerable involvement of Lundy is implicit in a request to Trinity House from the Board of Customs for the use of part of their land to build a preventive station on the island. The proprietor would not grant a lease as he was trying to sell the island, and Trinity House proved no more sympathetic, so the plan came to nothing. Doubtless this was a relief to the then owner's bailiff, a man of doubtful probity, and the others who were using Lundy as a convenient transit point for contraband.

The Trinity House agent was responsible for Lundy, and also for two lighthouses then at Bideford Bar (Braunton). He was resident at Bideford, and so was allowed £40 per annum expenses for visiting the island in addition to his salary of £80. To this was added £30 for the supervision of Bideford, a percentage as Collector of Light Dues which amounted to around £40, as well as a small sum as agent for pensioners of some £7. It was a much sought-after post.

James Cornish was installed as the principal keeper who, with his wife, occupied the ground floor accommodation, while the assistant keeper, William Rawle, and his family lived on the upper floor. Both were employed at a salary of £70 per year, with a £10 annual bonus. With two lights to be attended in three-hour shifts, the work for the keepers must have been arduous, and in addition they complained that they had to carry spring water from the island well a distance of 914 m (1000 yards) to their quarters. The enclosure to the east would have allowed the keepers to grow produce and to keep pigs (then an important part of any household economy). At that time there was no regular boat service from the mainland and no shop on the island, although some fresh produce could be obtained from the farmer. Pilot boats waited at Lundy for incoming ships which gave some contact with the outside world; the crews often carried letters.

At the time the lighthouse was completed the island was for sale, since the new owner was in need of money to settle his late father's debts. Trinity House was the first outside organisation to have an installation on Lundy, and the addition of two families to the small and isolated island community would have been an event of great significance. One account (Lysons and Lysons 1822) states that there were only two houses apart from the light keepers' quarters, and that

"The island abounds with rabbits, the shooting and catching of which forms the principal employment of the inhabitants: the rabbits are shot chiefly for their skins, and the birds, which are chiefly puffins, for their feathers".

### Excerpts from Trinity House Ledgers (THGLA, 1819-20)

**1819**

12 May. Mr Daniel Alexander. Paid for the advance on account of Light House Building at Lundy: £650

9 June. Paid Capt Lewin and Capt Gooch the Expenses of their Journey to the Island to fix the Site of the Lighthouse: £62.8.0.

December. Paid to Reed & Raggett. Lundy Light. 486 galls of Sperm Oil supplied. £159.0.3.

**1820**

12 August. George Robinson for the Lanthorn, Lamps, Reflectors, Stoves etc. £1987.16.6.

7-14 December. To Joseph Nelson the Contractor for the balance of his account for building the Light House as settled by Mr Phillips the surveyor £2560.19.0.

Oil supplied in the year to 31.12.1820 : 611 galls £199.12.1.

Thomas Grant for disbursements for Half a Year to 30 September 1820:

| | |
|---|---|
| Salary to 2 Light keepers £ | 84.19.00 |
| Rent of Storehouse | 03.10.06 |
| Hire of vessel to convey stores | 05.00.00 |
| Freight & carriage of sundries | 04.17.11 |
| Stationery, stamps and postage | 02.07.04 |
| Travelling expenses James Cornish | 15.00.00 |
| Ironmonger and Brazier | 19.14.09 |
| Gratuity to Mr McDonnel [agent for Vere Hunt] for assistance during the Works | 21.00.00 |
| Lodging for Light keepers during the completion of their dwelling | 02.02.00 |
| Salary as Agent [Thos Grant] | 118.17.00 |
| Expenses in visiting the Island | 23.06.00 |
| Compensation for his services during the erection of the Light | 105.00.00 |
| Allowance of £3 per month for the conveyance of stores | 09.00.00 |
| Extra travelling expenses | 14.10.00 |
| W & S Jones for a Achromatic telescope, case, etc. | 09.00.00 |

**1821**

| | |
|---|---|
| 25 September Cottage building | 395.02.00 |
| December Coals | 28.03.00 |
| Bags for ditto, Mops and Brushes | 10.16.03 |
| Oil supplied one year to December, 608 galls | 177.08.02 |

**1822**

| | |
|---|---|
| Sir Aubrey de Vere Hunt. Remuneration for lodgings for the Workmen during the erection of the Buildings. | 158.15.01 |

The lighthouse personnel were the only inhabitants not dependent on the proprietor. Once the lighthouse was established, periodic visits were made by the Elder Brethren and representatives of various Trinity House committees, who called on the proprietor if he was on the island. They inspected the lighthouse establishment, and arranged for supplies of oil, coal and other heavy necessities to be brought in by tender annually. Domestic supplies were, presumably, brought in by contract with local boatmen, but there is no information about this in the early years of working.

# Chapter 2
## Fog, landslips and Heaven: 1822–39

There would seem to have been either a drop in the rate of shipping casualties or, more probably, a deficit in reports, with a two-year gap before another wreck was recorded. The *Fame* packet was on her way from Bristol to Cork, but when she was stranded on the island in February 1822, all her crew survived. De Vere Hunt's bailiff wrote to him (Limerick Archive 1821–27) that:

> "There was several bails of cloath and leather brought ashore hear by us and the people of the island. I was advised by several people to claim a salvage on them, which they said was the one half as this being a free island. So the captin and I had a contest about it, as I toald him he should never take it off untill your honour should have the one half. So we boath left it to the settlement of Mr Grant and he would allow me nothing as the lives of the crew was saved."

Over the years many claims were made of rights to salvage or wreck on the very shaky basis of Lundy's supposed exemption from British laws, but in this case Grant evidently applied the law that no salvage could be claimed from a wrecked vessel if any kind of living thing had survived the accident. This letter, interestingly, was sent via the anti-smuggling preventive vessel.

Mannix, De Vere Hunt's bailiff, wrote again in 1823 about the wreck of a brig bound from Cork to Newport (*Ibid*):

> "…a great misfortune happened hear on the 30th October last. An Irish brig called the Marriston [*Morreston*] was wrecked hear and 25 persons drowned, besides 250 pigs. The captin and three men saved their lives on a part of the mast but one of the men died after he came ashore and we buried him and another man that was picked up on the island. We could save none of the wreck; she went to pieces."

In April 1825 he sent report of another wreck, the *Commerce* (*Ibid*):

> "Sir, we have a ship wreck on the Island, a very large Brig from Jersey called the Comas [*Commerce*], registered 154 tuns. She struck on the south end at the Shutter Rock on the morning of the 14th [April]. The crew was all saved, and the moast of the sails and rigging and all the valuable things that was in her. She was insured at Loydes and the materials are send to Ilfracombe. The captain is still on the island logging [lodging] at the light house, but the men are all gone home to Sunderland as they belonged there. Our men was three days saving the wreck etc…"

### Melancholy Shipwreck

Cork. The *Morreston* …left this harbour on the morning of Tuesday 29th ult., with a cargo of pigs; a crew consisting of the captain, pilot, four seamen and a boy, and seven passengers. She was accompanied by the *George the Fourth* steam-packet for the entire of that day, the wind and weather favourable; but wanting stern-sails she was unable to keep up with the *George the Fourth*, or the melancholy catastrophe which we are about to relate might have been avoided, as she would have reached Newport before the storm commenced. Captain Brown, of the steam packet, describes the gale as the most tremendous that was ever experienced in the navigation between Cork and Bristol. The light at Lundy Island, which the *Morreston* had passed, could not be seen at 200 yards distance. The *Morreston* was bearing away for Cork when she was blown right on the island, and at a distance of not more than 20 yards from the shore, at ten p.m. she struck.

The scene that ensued cannot be described. One of the survivors has arrived in this city; he is the pilot…He stated that four persons only came on shore, one of whom died immediately. The Captain and boy remain at Lundy Island and this man came over in the *Marquis of Anglesey* packet…he had clung to a plank, and was nearly washed off it several times, but still held on, while another person, whom he could not distinguish…was struck off and met a watery grave.

(The Times 1823)

That was the last account of a wreck given by Mannix who, his iniquities having been drawn to the attention of his employer, left Lundy in 1827.

It was not long before two problems manifested themselves that were to dog Trinity House for many years. Because the cliffs around the area of the landing place are composed of shale, there are frequent landslips. These had been causing damage to the quay, path, and storehouses that was often very severe. Repairs were carried out in 1823, evidently not for the first time, and Grant was obliged to send workmen over to reconstruct the road before the oil and other stores could be transported up to the lighthouse. Trinity House tried to limit the expenses by proposing that the island owner, De Vere Hunt, should contribute to the cost of repairs, but he replied that he was committed to a sale of the island, and was not therefore in a position to enter a new agreement. He was evidently not aware that Trinity House had previously carried out all the repairs to the road.

With this a recurring problem, lesser repairs were usually carried out by the islanders, but early in 1826 major repairs were once again needed at the landing place, the road, and some of the buildings. It was September before Trinity House sent Nelson back to the island with eighteen men to carry out the work. He was also instructed to build a pier. Since the Trinity House marker stone carries the date 1819, it seems probable that 'pier' referred to the southern curved extension to the quay that is shown in the plan of 1842, or to a quay extension that was subsequently lost. De Vere Hunt's bailiff wrote that Nelson repaired the quay, and the road from the beach which was in very bad condition. He then built two or three small houses in the lighthouse yard, and a small storehouse on the quay. As early as the following December there was yet another landslip, and Grant had to report that considerable damage had been done to the new storehouse and walls, and that the fallen rocks blocked the road leading up to the lighthouse once more.

An even more serious matter was that the light itself was sometimes obscured by fog. Lieutenant Crosbie, commander of the Revenue cruiser, *Hawke*, wrote to Trinity House in July 1824 (THGLA 1824), claiming that:

> "...the Journals of the Light keepers will prove that nearly nine months of the year the Light House and upper part of the island is cap'd with Fogs, more particularly the top of the Light House when the wind is...westward, and by westerly gales, the spray (beyond belief) goes over the top of the Light House [sic]...a height about 600 feet, and during winter leaves behind a crystallised salt and the glass of the lamps becomes so covered that they require washing with brushes, consequently that the Upper Light very frequently is rendered useless..."

The Old Light capped by fog (courtesy of R. Derek Sach)

He also complained that the space between the upper and lower lights was insufficient to distinguish between the two, and suggested that a new lighthouse should be built in a position WSW of the existing one.

Thomas Grant was ordered to go to Lundy and report on the matter, and his opinion was that the complaint should be dismissed. He held that Lundy was no more prone to fogs than other parts of the coast of similar elevation, and stated that no brush was ever used to remove any crystallised deposits or other matter from the glass. He maintained that, contrary to Lieutenant Crosbie's opinion, the lighthouse had been highly praised. Further, the light keepers' journal showed that fog had been recorded at the Lighthouse for a total of only sixty-four days in the previous eleven months. Crosbie's claim would seem to have been exaggerated, so that it was not taken seriously in the light of Grant's opinion. Presumably a fog incidence of approximately one day in five was either not calculated or not given weight. It was tartly decreed that no one other than Trinity House personnel should be allowed to read the lighthouse journals. In fact, the complaint reflected the fact that Trinity House was unaware of the singular character of fogs on Lundy, when the plateau is often capped by fog which renders the tower of the lighthouse invisible, while leaving the lower sidelands quite clear. Doubtless pride in the very fine building also had a part in the reluctance to admit that it was seriously flawed.

Further complaints were received that the upper and lower lights were not sufficiently distinct from one another, and that on one occasion the light had failed to revolve. This failure was denied by the keepers, but the deficiency of the relative positions of the lights was investigated, and various solutions proposed, even to the extent of considering a new lighthouse. A plan of the Trinity House plot was made to examine if this were practicable, but in the end it was decided that Nelson should carry out his own suggestion to move the lower light to ground level. A survey of the Trinity House land was ordered and a plan made, which showed that a block had been added against the west wall of the lighthouse compound, which was used for "Coal House, Forge, Wash Houses etc".

Nelson was commissioned to build a new lantern room for the lower light at the base of the tower, which would then be 21.6 m (71 ft) below the upper light, instead of 9.1 m (30 ft). On 3rd August 1829 the new lower light was exhibited for the first time. This brought the total number of burners to thirteen: four in the upper light and nine in the lower, all with reflectors. At the same time Nelson built a small additional barrack for the men who would land with, and carry up, the stores. The building of the lantern room also indicates that the offices had previously been removed from the southeast corner of the compound to where the low light lantern room now is, and it was necessary to move them once again. All was completed and in good order by August 1829, except that the surrounding wall of the keepers' garden was only built of earth partially faced with stones. Mr Nelson suggested that he could put it in condition with more earth for five pounds, so that it would stand for another few years. Apart from that, it was remarked: "The rats swarm and are most destructive to every thing growing on the island" (THGLA 1829).

A lesser hazard experienced from time to time was the crashing of birds against the lantern. With small birds on migration no damage was done, but in 1827 a flock of wild ducks hit the panes of glass and broke two of them, which necessitated emergency repairs before replacement windows could be sent out to the island. The seven dead ducks that were picked up from the gallery were doubtless a welcome addition to the light keepers' diet.

After the trial of using the donkeys for transporting loads, it was decided that they should be replaced by manpower because the process took too long. There had also been theft of the coals before they could be moved up to the lighthouse. The carrying capacity of the two donkeys was small anyway, and an experiment was carried out to determine what quantities of oil or coal one man could take up in a day. Even this experiment had to wait on repairs to the road, blocked by yet another landfall. Meanwhile, De Vere Hunt had failed in his efforts to sell the island and he offered it to Trinity House, an offer which was promptly declined.

It would be difficult to try to assess the effectiveness of the lighthouse in reducing the loss of lives at sea. Nothing could prevent the loss of sailing ships at the mercy of violent weather, a faulty vessel, or an ignorant, negligent or drunken crew. Added problems are the paucity of records of wrecks in the eighteenth and early nineteenth centuries, and a lack of figures for the volume of shipping using the channel. The comparison of the period 1750–1820 when one wreck is recorded for every five years, with one wreck in every one and a half years during the first nine years of the lighthouse cannot be construed as a criticism of the lighthouse itself. Indeed, the presence of the light keepers on watch most probably resulted in a few more wrecks being recorded.

One man died when the schooner *IO* of Jersey on her way to Cardiff collided with a brigantine near the South Hole (Devil's Limekiln) on 25th April 1828. This is near the Shutter Rock, and would confirm the earlier name of Shatter Rock as the site of several wrecks. Thirteen of the nineteen souls on board *La Jeune Emma* lost their lives when she was wrecked off Rat Island in November of 1828, among them a niece of the Empress Josephine. The *Francis Anne* was on her way from Bristol to St Ives in 1829 when she struck submerged rocks at Rat Island and was also a total loss. All of the crew of the brig *Hope* were lost on 27th March 1829, except for the captain who was rescued by a skiff.

> The two pilots from Ilfracombe, who rendered their assistance to the Russian squadron, have been remunerated with the sum of £300 [approximately £20,000 today]. On the pilots' arriving at the mooring of the squadron, they found the vessels in great distress, and immediately cut their cables and proceeded up channel to Kingroad. The pilots have been retained on board the fleet, at a handsome salary. Considering the violence of the gale, it might be considered a providential interference that the vessels were not wrecked on the numerous rocks by which they were surrounded.
>
> (The Times 1828)

After many tribulations, De Vere Hunt finally succeeded in selling Lundy in 1830 to a Mr Matravers of Wiltshire and a Mr Stiffe of Gloucestershire, about whom little is known. Just after that there was a dramatic event in 1831 when the tower of the lighthouse was struck by lightning. Grant forwarded to Trinity House the keepers' own description of the event (THGLA 1831a):

"...the lightning entered at the Door at the Head of the Stairs, which was open, that it struck the Hand Rail of the Stairs and fortunately passed out through the Lower Door (which was likewise open) without doing any Injury, and that a man who was on the stairs received a slight shock as the Fluid passed him...the Appearance of the Inside of the Tower was that of its being on fire, and that a body of fire was observed to rush out of the Lower Door, and passed the Observer with a loud and peculiar Noise".

It was decided that the Board would (*Ibid*)

"...take into Consideration the Propriety of fixing a Conductor at this and other of the Corporation's Light Houses".

Some of the horror of shipwreck is described by a writer for *The Exeter Flying Post* (1833) in March of 1833 in the case of the *Erin*:

"…we fear this ship is gone to the bottom, as nothing has been heard of her since the 21st ult [February], when she was seen near Lundy island, in great distress…her sails dragging in the water, and her crew in the rigging, where they were making signals, and uttering loud cries for help. Fire doors, painted and varnished, have been washed on shore near Bideford, and a brass rail and a ladder belonging to a steamer have been picked up at Milford, for which port she was making when last seen. It is understood there were above 30 passengers on board…the crew consisted of 22…"

Two ships sighted her, but no explanation is offered for their failure to provide assistance. Some two months earlier the smack *Unity* had gone to the bottom, but there are no wrecks recorded after that until 1835, when the *Rapid* came to grief on the east side though all her crew survived.

Lundy lighthouse counted as a shore station and so families were accommodated, although nothing is known of the number of children there in the 1820s and 1830s except that Rawle had at least one daughter. But it was a land station with just a farm, no church or school; even telegrams, or establishing the correct time, had to wait on the arrival of a ship. Neither was there a doctor, or any medical resources. The only way of summoning help was to light a beacon in the hope that it would be seen from the mainland and acted upon, and that the weather would allow helpers to make the crossing to the island. If the patient was well enough to travel, he or she could wait for the next homeward-bound vessel to call at the island, and beg or buy a passage to the mainland. There was no island boat, as vessels were chartered when needed, usually from Clovelly, and the Trinity House supply boats came infrequently. So it seems entirely reasonable that the keepers would ask Trinity House to provide a medicine chest — a request that was not fulfilled before it had been repeated several times. A request was also made for bibles and prayer books, as there was no church or minister.

The surviving letters written to De Vere Hunt by Mannix give an interesting vignette of island life at the time. The population, apart from the light keepers and their dependants, consisted of Mannix, his wife and daughter, three labourers and two women. The island economy depended on the farming of livestock, with some arable cultivation for feed, domestic needs, and sale to ships crews. This was augmented by the sale of rabbit skins, sea-bird feathers and eggs, trade with the crews of ships, and a small income from haulage and other services to Trinity House. Butter and cheese were the main products, which were sold on the mainland, to ships, and on the island, although there were constant complaints from the island customers that Mannix overcharged them. Supplies and post were irregular; the most regular visitors were the Bristol Channel pilots from Pill in Somerset, who waited at Lundy for incoming vessels. They sometimes carried letters, but were also engaged in smuggling and, it is suspected, theft, in collusion with some of the islanders.

1831 was a year when serious rioting took place in Bristol following the rejection of the Reform Bill in the House of Commons, and several public buildings were burned down. Mr Stiffe wrote to Trinity House (THGLA 1831b):

> "...concerning his intention, owing to the disturbed state of that part of the country, to remove with his family to Lundy Island for a time, and requesting therefore to be allowed to use the cottage adjoining the Lighthouse. Resolved that the accommodation requested by Mr Stiffe be granted provided that an apartment, as requisite, be provided

at any time for the use of the Elder Brethren, or the Agent, when detained upon the island."

Whether Stiffe availed himself of this is not recorded, but it indicates that any other accommodation on the island was in full use, and that the seriousness of the disorder in Bristol was such that a gentleman would consider putting his family in a small two-roomed cottage with no facilities. It is thought that the only accommodation on the island at that time was the farmhouse (in two sections) built by Sir John Borlase Warren circa 1775–76, and some semi-derelict housing at the old castle used by labourers.

Lieutenant Denham surveyed Lundy for the Admiralty in 1832, drew a splendid map, and wrote sailing directions (Denham 1832), where he described the island as:

> "...in the material character of an asylum, the island of Lundy is invaluable...it offers a sheltered anchorage for any-sized ships in 'easy water'...with means of replenishing live stock, provender, vegetables and water...a valuable warning beacon to those who are venturing and groping under doubtful reckoning...the Light-house is a beautifully proportioned tower of granite...the upper lamps are elevated five hundred and sixty-seven feet above low water level, producing an intermittent light (appearing bright for ten seconds, at intervals of twenty-two seconds obscuration) — visible, in clear weather, to an eye ten feet above the water, thirty-one miles, and ranging round the compass. The lower light...only ranges in the western aspect, between the points of S. by E. and N. by W., exhibiting a fixed light; thereby distinguishing Lundy lights from all others; it may be seen twenty-nine miles; and, when hovering under the western side of the island at night to cheat the ebb, it becomes a rule, that you are clear of all straggling rocks (even the Hen and Chickens) so long as the lower light is seen over the cliff...the island generally harbours a relief of pilot skiffs. The fact of any-sized vessels being enabled to lie under the island, sheltered from the prevailing winds, cannot be too highly esteemed by the vast commercial and shipping interests which give rise to such extensive shipping intercourse as the Bristol Channel waters bear up and down; more especially as no other roadstead exists wherein a loaded or sharp-built ship can lie afloat except Kingroad [Bristol] which is situated eighty miles above Lundy."

Periodic visits were made by Trinity House committees, who had the responsibility of reporting on all aspects of the lighthouse. This included its function, personnel, and the condition of the station as a whole. In February 1834 the report read as follows (THGLA 1834):

> "At noon, blowing strong from S.W. with thick weather and rain, weighed from St Mary's Sound [Scilly] for Lundy, under treble reefed sails. On Friday at 8 a.m. landed at Lundy, raining incessantly and very thick weather. This establishment was clean and in good repair, the lantern inside and out, the gallery, railing, frames, and sashes of doors and windows and all the outside woodwork, were finished painting in July last. The leak in the roof of the dwelling continues. The door from the Lantern to the Gallery is decayed and requires a new one. Iron would be preferable, as it is small

and much exposed; application was made for three outer windows to be fitted in the
S.W. recesses — the rain at present forces its way under the sashes and runs down the
Tower, in considerable quantities. There are 13 lamps in use and 8 spare ones; three
of which were at Bideford for repair, and the whole of them are much worn, a new
set should be furnished, and those in use sent to London for repair. The medicine
chest formerly recommended has not been furnished, and is much required. The
person in charge of the island requested permission for some of his men being
allowed to sleep in a Shed belonging to the Light House, until they erected a building
next spring. This was refused, but as he was desirous application should be made to
the Board, he was informed, if their sanction was obtained it would be communicated
to him through Mr Grant."

---

### Parliamentary report on lighthouses, 1834

**1829**

Expenditure on improvements and Low Light removed to foot of tower £1010
12s 5d

[Approximately £75,000 today]

**1831**

Agent for Lundy & Bideford

Bideford Bar 2 lighthouses opened 10 Nov 1820

| | |
|---|---|
| Salary Agent | £80 |
| Agent Bideford | £30 |
| Collector of Light Duties | £44 16s 07d |
| Agent for pensioners | £07 10s 00 |
| Collector of Customs | – |
| | -------------- |
| | £162 06s 07d |

Expenses for visiting Lundy £40
(no tender employed. 8 visits in 1833)

**1833**

No of burners 13

Annual consumption of oil 603 [galls]

2 Keepers, salaries and allowances £80

(National Archives 1834)

---

Not long after this Matravers and Stiffe sold the island to William Hudson
Heaven, gentleman, of Bristol. Possibly the man in charge of the island was his
manager and Heaven had possession of the island from 1834, two years before
the legal deed was completed.

Heaven intended to use the island for shooting and as a summer resort
for his family, unlike previous owners who either leased it to others, or left a
bailiff to manage it. He soon had an elegant house, the Villa, built for his own
occupation (the present Millcombe), enlarged the farmhouse, and built cottages
within the castle for labourers. He improved the road from the beach to the

plateau and built a new section through Millcombe Valley, so that horses and carts could be used for haulage from the landing beach to the Villa and the plateau, and the ladies could use a carriage. Heaven also contracted a boat from Clovelly to provide a regular service to the island, which was all the more necessary as he had given up his own boat, and needed to import building materials and goods to sustain his workforce.

He invited Trinity House to share the cost of the boat hire, which would also be of service for the lighthouse, and this proposal was agreed on. The shortage of accommodation was also a problem, and Heaven obtained permission to use the Cottage in the Garden (the agent's cottage), though his proposal for their co-operation in building the new road was put on Trinity House's back burner. It seems that relations between Heaven's agent, William Malbon, and the light keepers deteriorated sharply for some reason. In May of 1838 Malbon locked up the well which the keepers had been accustomed to use, and as a result it seems that Heaven was dispossessed of the cottage in the Garden. Malbon retaliated by refusing to haul the empty oil tins from the lighthouse to the store on the quay, and locked up the store to which the keepers should have had access. All this was against the terms of Heaven's agreement with Trinity House, and he had to give assurances of amendment, while Trinity House took back possession of the cottage, allowing only temporary use of it from time to time for Heaven's own guests.

William Rawle was found to be in ill health and considered not to be fully competent, and so, after nineteen years on the island, he left with a pension of £31 10s per year. His application for an increase in the amount was refused. He was replaced by John Phelps, aged 39, who arrived in February 1839. Shortly after that, James Cornish asked to leave and to receive his pension, which was granted on the same terms as Rawle, because of his "Rheumatism and Spasms, and general appearance" (THGLA 1839a) Samuel Boulder was appointed in his place, and Phelps was promoted to principal keeper. By that time Heaven had completed his house and Malbon had left the island, which was leased to Robert Rowles for seven years. His lease comprised all the island, with the exception of an area in the southeast around the new Villa, reserved for the Heaven family, and the land leased to Trinity House.

Shortly after Phelps' arrival Thomas Grant died suddenly. Although the Board received two applications for the post from Bideford written on the day of Grant's death, Trinity House took the opportunity to rationalise supervision of Lundy by transferring the agency to Lieutenant Mott at Milford Haven, from where all supplies and communications would be provided by the tender stationed there. It was also decided (THGLA 1839b) that:

"…a Steam vessel of sufficient size and power should be provided to be stationed at Milford, and that an efficient Sailing Tender should also be stationed at the intended store at Cardiff, and that under such arrangements…the several Agencies in the Bristol and St. George's Channels from the Rivers Usk and Avon to the South Stack inclusive be consolidated as opportunities may offer and placed in charge of the Superintendent at Milford…Ordered that measures be forthwith taken for securing… Two marine steam engines of 50 Horse power…from Messrs Bolton & Watt…the Board to determine the size of the Vessel…"

The Heaven family villa in Millcombe (Heaven archive)

The agent's cottage (now Stoneycroft)

No notice had been given to Heaven, who objected to the sudden cancellation of his contract with Trinity House for supplying the lighthouse, particularly as he had recently engaged a vessel from Bideford to serve the island for twelve months at a cost of £60. Accordingly, Trinity House paid him their due, and also £150 for services provided during the previous twelve months. At the same time, he was asked to continue the service of hauling stores from the landing place to the lighthouse, which he agreed to do on an *ad hoc* rather than a contract basis. Pending the new arrangements being put into place, a Mr Rodd acted as Trinity House agent at Bideford and Lundy.

# Chapter 3

## PROFESSOR FARADAY ADVISES: 1839–49

The efficiency of the light was still in question, but the wheels of official action turned very slowly, perhaps out of some reluctance to admit that there were shortcomings with this magnificent new lighthouse. In April 1839, matters were considered by the visiting committee (THGLA 1839c).

"In October 1837...the painting and whitewashing of the whole [tower and dwellings] were recommended, and last year Estimates from three parties were obtained...but the amounts tendered were so exorbitant, that the Committee declined to entertain them, contemplating...a measure which will hereafter be submitted, for effecting such reparations...that the materials and labour to be employed thereon will also be superior:- it is therefore proposed to execute those works in the current year, and further it seems desirable to the Committee that the external parts of the Buildings and Tower should be painted white. In reporting upon this establishment, the Committee claim the attention of the Board to the light exhibited therefrom...its great altitude and consequent liability to fog and haze, render it expedient that the light should be of the first magnitude: this object, it is considered, is not obtainable by the operation of one Reflector passing in review, and therefore that a multiplication of them is necessary at this station...the duration of light is the same at the South Bishop and nearly so that of Scilly; if the Board concur in opinion with the Committee, that this light should be strengthened, they recommend that 15 or 18 Reflectors be arranged upon three faces and that the revolution be altered to six minutes."

In July another visit was carried out by the Committee of the Bristol Channel, who submitted their recommendations.

"...the lantern should be painted inside and out, the exterior of the Tower be painted white, but not the Buildings, the interior of the Tower be whitewashed, and that of the Lower Light room painted...The road which belongs to the Corporation (but only that from its junction with that recently made by Mr Heaven) should be put in order and kept so...In the lantern are 8 lamps and Reflectors on an octagonal frame, which makes its revolution once in three minutes; in the lower light room, which is 70 feet below the other, are five Lamps and Reflectors, facing from NNW to WSW and the whole are clean and in good order, and the Establishment altogether of the first-rate character, the Tower and Buildings being of the best and most suitable description. But as a more powerful light has been recommended at this important and very advanced situation at the entrance of the great trading Estuary of the Severn, we think that a revolving Light of 18 or 21 Reflectors, say 6 or 7 on each face, and one of those faces to be shaded red, as at the Flambro, and to make a complete revolution in 6 minutes, showing its light once in two minutes, will have the desired effect, and distinguish it from the other lights in its vicinity, particularly if the lower light should be retained; but even this may, perhaps, be then dispensed with..."

Further (THGLA 1839d),

"...the Oil Cellar [should be] whitewashed and the oil cisterns fresh painted, and the Lamps in the Lantern and Light room to be japan'd or made of brass. The interiors of the residences to be painted, the passages and pantries plastered and coloured, and an external shutter made to Phelps' Bedroom. The Outbuildings or offices should have Zinc Spouts all round the roof to catch the rain-water that can be collected, as one-third of the keeper's time is employ'd in bringing water from the Spring which, he says, is nearly 1,000 yards off. The interiors of the outbuildings should be whitewashed and the Garden Walls made good and higher all round...The Agent's cottage, which has two rooms in it, should be plastered, painted, and refitted for his use, and have two new fire grates put in them, or else should be taken down altogether, and not left to go to ruin and decay as it now is...The Store, of which the key was readily obtained, required a trifling repair over the door, and its wall is cracked by a settlement, the Landing Place is very good."

In the summer of 1840 maintenance works were put in hand. That time the Committee to the Seven Stones visited Lundy (THGLA 1839–40).

"[They] landed the Stores and Painters...the Old Wall which encloses the North and East part of the Corporation's premises should be rebuilt, and carried high enough to keep the sheep out of the keepers' Gardens - this wall is now in a most dilapidated state, hollow'd out by Rat Burrows, and also to widen the road from Peeping Corner [later the Battlements] to the Trinity Road, at present it is dangerous for the horses in dragging up the Stores, the Tenant, Mr Rawle, will undertake to do this for £10...fit double windows in the Tower where they have not already been done, the well to be cleaned out and compoed, and drains made to take the rain water from the roof to the Tanks, a pump to be fitted to the sink of the Upper House, as at present they stop the water-pipe at bottom, and make a cistern of the roof, to save the trouble of fetching water from the sink of the Lower House, which has a pump. One set of furniture required here for the Assistant Keeper, a single man, but expects his sister from the Lizard to live with him, some alteration to the drains from the privvies to be made outside, complains of the badness of the cylinders."

Evidently some measures had been taken, albeit late, to conserve water. The use of horses for dragging loads draws attention to Heaven's improvement of the Beach Road, which met the old steep track where the Battlements now are. Trinity House had a right of way on the old path from the landing place to the lighthouse, but since the Corporation had failed to respond to Heaven's invitation to divide the work and the expense of improving it and building the new section, he forbade them to use it. They had, however, put markers along their route to the lighthouse to mark their right of way, of which one remains at the top of St John's Valley.

Trinity House made a decision in October of 1840 (THGLA 1840a) that:

"a Catadioptric Light of the First Character, with a new First Class Lantern be prepared for the Upper Light in this Tower, to revolve in 16 minutes, in line of the present apparatus for exhibiting that Light, and that the Light at the base of the Tower be improved by fixing the Parabolic Reflectors on a concave frame to extend as far as the Light can be seen seaward from the opening in that Light Room."

The Trinity House engineer, James Walker, advised that the tower would have to be adapted before it could accommodate a larger, fourteen-feet lantern, and that (THGLA 1840b)

> "by adding another course of granite over the present cornice 15 ins thick and projecting 1 foot beyond the present finishing course, a 14 feet lantern may be fixed with a gallery 2 ft 9 ins in width...the course will contain 300 cubic feet [of granite]..."

This was agreed, and in January 1841 the Board approved the provision of a revolving light on the dioptric principle and arrangements were made for the Trinity House steamer *Argus* to ship the new apparatus to the island. That meant a significant change from the use of metal reflectors to optical lenses, with reflectors for the upper light which, for a revolving light, were mounted on a frame. The lenses, developed by Fresnel, consisted of a bull's-eye lens surrounded by concentric rings of prismatic glass which refracted the light into a horizontal beam. The iron pedestal and lantern were shipped first, followed by the delivery of nine polyzonal lenses and 363 mirrors. It was ordered that the old light apparatus should be taken for use at St Anne's Point lighthouse.

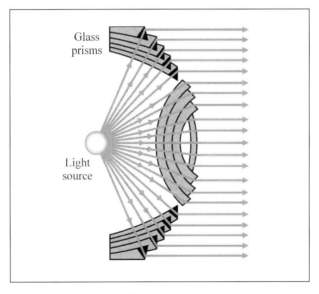

Catadioptric apparatus

With heavy machinery to be transported up to the lighthouse, the advantages of using the new road became ever more evident, and Walker, the Trinity House engineer, approached Mr Heaven about terms. Heaven was prepared to allow its use in return for Trinity House undertaking the necessary existing, and all future, repairs. The immediate work consisted of repairs to the quay and wall, estimated at £300, and Trinity House also wanted "To have the made road continued up to the Lighthouse, over the boggy fields [plan not included in illustration], the length of which is 968 yards, to properly form and stone which, it is estimated will cost £250 to £300" (THGLA 1842a). Trinity House's counter offer was that Heaven should carry out the work, for which they would meet half the cost, and that an annual sum of £5 to £10 would be allowed for Heaven keeping the whole length of the road in repair. Not unnaturally Heaven rejected this, and the negotiations went back and forth until August 1842, when it was agreed that Trinity House would pay Heaven for carrying out the necessary repairs to the section of the road G to H and the wall. In return for use of the new road, they would pay £10 per annum for general repairs, and in addition would undertake work made necessary by landslips or other accidents. These terms were finally agreed on the 2nd August, in time for the transportation of the new apparatus.

The distinguished scientist, Professor Faraday, was called in by Trinity House to advise on the new light. He recommended a new method of constructing the frame and fixing the mirrors, and subsequently went to inspect the work at Messrs Wilkins, who had obtained the contract. His report (THGLA 1830, 1841) said that:

"Having examined the arrangement of a whole division of the Mirrors of the Lens Light Apparatus ...according to the mode of suspending and attaching them which he recommended for adoption in a former Report. He believes he has every reason to be satisfied with the result of the plan, and that so far as he can see in no point does it come short of the advantages he had anticipated from it...Mr Wilkins is fully satisfied with the strength of the suspension and facility of workmanship and adjustment. That he is also satisfied with the effect of the extra row of mirrors which he has introduced between the revolving Lenses and the upper part of the system of fixed mirrors. The professor then offers some observations having for object an improved mode of selecting the Mirrors to be placed in the most effective part of the Apparatus Viz the first tier above the Refractors. And concludes by suggesting that the ribs of the apparatus which in obedience to orders that it should be made exactly in the manner of the French are of wrought iron, may with advantage be constructed of cast bronze."

The new apparatus was installed in October of 1842, as Wilkins (who was the engineer of the construction firm) wrote from Lundy (THGLA 1842b) and

"...reported his having completed the dioptric Apparatus at the Lundy Light with the Refractors placed at the Angle directed by Mr Faraday and removed the temporary light machinery and exhibited the new Light on the evening of the 31st Ultimo [October], Also that the improved Light from 9 Argand Lamps and Parabolic Reflectors was exhibited in the Lower Light Room at that station on the evening of the 12th Instant [November]. That the mirrors to complete the Catadioptric Apparatus in the Upper Lantern were being placed in the manner directed by Mr Faraday's instructions. Mr Wilkins then suggests that the Board may probably deem it necessary to provide further assistance for maintaining a perpetual Watch in these Lanterns. The Board was hereupon of Opinion that the present Light-keepers and their families [not employed by Trinity House and therefore unpaid] are fully sufficient for the purpose."

By March 1843 all the work had been completed, and the pilots' opinion was reported to be that the light was both brilliant and powerful. The upper light revolved every two minutes, and the lower light was fixed and visible only from the westward.

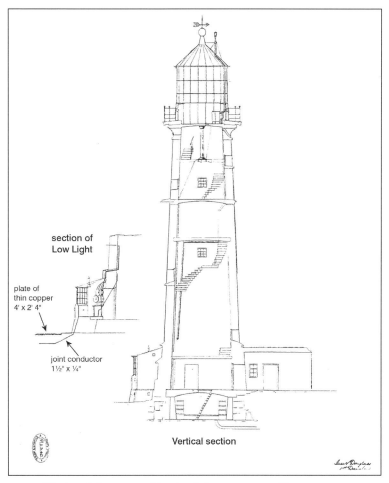

The low light at ground level and the reconstructed lantern room
(THEA No. 1340, 1863)

In the intervening years, how effective had the unimproved lighthouse been in reducing the number of shipwrecks on or near Lundy? Between the end of 1829 and August 1842 there are records of eleven wrecks. There was a one-year gap between the *Rapid* in 1835 and the *Abbotsford*, which was actually carrying a pilot when she struck. She was refloated and taken to Ilfracombe, although said then to be in a sinking state. Also in 1836 an unidentified Danish ship sprang a leak and sank west of Lundy; the crew were able to scramble into their boat, which drifted, and fortunately they were picked up. Mr Heaven's agent wrote (Heaven Archive 1836):

> "...a boat and seven men were floating about the West side of the island...I had the boat launched and myself and three others went to their assistance and towed them on shore. They had been out a day and a night without any provisions...I gave them each a glass of rum and rigged them out with dry clothes, and after breakfast they went to bed. They are Danes and can speak but little English...She sprung a leak at 7 o'clock in the morning of the 6th instant about 10 or 12 miles to the West of the island. The pilots cannot think how they could have been saved, for it blew a hurricane last night. I have bought their boat...for One pound ten shillings which...is a bargain."

The hazard of a sudden change of wind direction was evident when in 1838 an un-named vessel "belonging to Shields" was anchored in the bay when the wind suddenly veered to the east; she was driven onto the beach and broke up.

There was a gap (either in wrecks or in records) until 1841, when the *Sarah* sank and was abandoned off the island. In the same year the *Eliza* suffered the same fate; the crew was rescued from their boat by the *Susan* and were landed at Appledore. In 1842, before the installation of the new lantern, the *Mariner* suffered a total loss. The lighthouse would have made little difference in the case of a ship springing a leak, which was the cause of the sinking of the *Crescent* near Lundy Roads in June of 1842. Her crew took to the boats, and, as written in the *Exeter Flying Post* (1842):

> "...reached Lundy where they took shelter in the hole of a rock for two nights and a day, and we regret to say that although under such perilous circumstances and fatigue, the people of the island neither offered or rendered the sufferers the least assistance or served them with any provisions the whole time they were on the island. The Trinity steamer Argus took them off and landed them at Appledore, the captain hailing them with the greatest kindness and humanity."

It may be asked if the islanders actually knew the men were hidden in a cave, or even why they did not make their way to the farm or the lighthouse. Although the rate of losses was very slightly down compared with the period 1820–1829, the lack of data for traffic volume, weather, vessel quality and standard of seamanship prevents accurate comparisons.

Another recurrent problem at Lundy was the state of the garden or enclosure walls. In the beginning it was clear that 'garden' was used to refer to the lighthouse compound, but it is sometimes difficult to know whether later references are to those walls or the walls of the enclosure to the east, referred to as either Meadow Ground or Waste Ground (now The Paddock). The repairs recommended in the above report of 1840 were postponed to 1842, and then again in 1843 *sine die*. Another uncertainty in interpreting the minutes lies in references to the storehouses. The 1842 plan shows a storehouse at the junction of the old and new roads, and there are also references to one on or near the quay as well as to Mr Heaven's storehouse and the Trinity storehouse. Confusion may arise from the fact that these were rebuilt from time to time when damaged by rock falls. However, Heaven completed the repair of the road and wall in 1842, and was paid the agreed £300 for the work.

### Lundy: Return of revenue from lighthouse dues

|      | £Gross | £Commission | £Net | £Maintenance | £Surplus |
|------|--------|-------------|------|--------------|----------|
| 1820 | 1202.00.00 | 181.00.00 | 1021.00.00 | 746.00.00 | 275.00.00 |
| 1822 | 1464.12.08 | 276.19.00 | 1187.13.08 | 895.13.01 | 292.07.00 |
| 1823 | 1338.09.11 | 157.08.01 | 1181.01.10 | 608.08.01 | 572.13.09 |
| 1824 | 1294.15.08 | 151.03.04 | 1143.12.04 | 775.03.00 | 368.09.04 |
| 1825 | 1292.02.05 | 151.11.00 | 1139.11.05 | 710.17.05 | 428.14.00 |
| 1826 | 1424.04.01 | 163.18.01 | 1260.06.00 | 1407.18.09 | (147.12.09) |
| 1827 | 1344.04.07 | 154.01.11 | 1190.02.08 | 912.15.11 | 277.06.09 |
| 1828 | 1415.16.07½ | 163.03.10¼ | 1252.12.09¼ | 871.04.10 | 381.07.11¼ |
| 1832 | 1786.02.00¾ | 203.18.11¼ | 15882.03.01½ | 798.04.04 | 783.18.09½ |
| 1838 | 1783.11.09 | 94.07.01¾ | 1689.04.07¼ | 757.14.09 | 931.09.10 |
| 1839 | 1958.04.10½ | 103.18.00¾ | 1854.06.09¾ | 952.15.11 | 901.10.10¾ |
| 1840 | 2050.03.07½ | 108.14.11½ | 1941.08.08 | 808.18.06 | 1132.10.02 |
| 1841 | 1941.15.07½ | 106.05.11¾ | 1835.09.07¾ | 2547.03.09 | (711.14.01¼) |
| 1842 | 2078.16.11½ | 110.17.07¾ | 1967.19.03¾ | 739.07.03 | 1228.12.00¾ |
| 1843 | 2033.19.09½ | 108.01.05¾ | 1925.18.03¾ | 5042.04.09 | (3116.06.05½) |

The commission was paid as a % to the collector of dues, who was usually the Trinity House agent. The commission was not standard, but varied between stations. The % was reduced following the reduction in dues received.

- In 1826 there were building works and road repairs;
- In 1841 the lantern was enlarged and a larger light installed;
- In 1843 the upper light was replaced with a more advanced system.

(National Archives 1829, 1834, 1845)

On the morning of 11th January 1843, the revolving movement of the light stopped. PK Phelps reported Samuel Boulden for having deliberately stopped the apparatus, and Boulden was immediately removed from Lundy. William Westmoreland of Start light was appointed in his place, but begged not to go to Lundy because he was afraid that the exposed location of the island would be too severe for his delicate constitution. Accordingly, George Monk, who had been appointed to Start in Westmoreland's place, was sent to Lundy instead. Boulden was examined by the Committee in London but was unable to explain the circumstance. He was found guilty as charged and was dismissed from the service. He later made repeated efforts to clear himself and become reinstated, suggesting that he considered himself misjudged. Westmoreland then requested a transfer from his post because he objected to one of the other keeper's behaviour. However, before that he had been transferred from Nash to Start at his own request because of his health. But he had shot himself in the foot, as after he had refused Lundy, an enquiry was ordered into his suitability to remain as a light keeper.

Many lighthouses were far removed from churches, and the Reverend John Ashley's Bristol Channel Mission attempted to fill the gap. His diary between 1841 and 1843 has survived, and he found that relations between the light keepers and the islanders, and between the islanders themselves, were at a low ebb. Quite apart from being frequently frustrated in his attempts to make a landing, he appears to have found Lundy especially problematical. He wrote on 28th May 1842 (Revd Ashley Diary, 1841–43):

"Went on shore and visited the people at Mr Heaven's, the Farm House, and Light House — the people as before, all packed and torn with dissentions."

On 29th May, he continued:

"Went on shore for service at half past 10 on Lundy island. The Light Keeper, Phelps, with his wife, refused to attend because they would not enter a building with any other person on the Island. Such is the animosity that exists between them and has existed for upwards of 20 years past. There are not 2 persons on the island that will speak to each other or cross to each other's side of the island. However, I had a better attendance than on the former occasion, and the farmer [Rowles] who never attended service on the island before came twice today, and on the second occasion brought his wife and all his family."

On 30th May 1842 he wrote:

"Went on shore to visit the people at the Castle who did not come to service yesterday. They appear to be very indifferent to every thing serious and living in sin. Gave them a Testament...One of our men...was given permission to go to the Island,

and in taking wild fowls eggs he fell from the rocks. He is much bruised but I believe has sustained no serious injury."

On 3rd October 1842, after a testing climb when landed on the West Side,

"We had a delightful evening on the Island, but before we could do anything we were obliged to beg for a fire to warm ourselves and some food to strengthen us, as we were sinking with hunger — both of which were kindly supplied to us at Mr Heaven's. The bell was rung for service, and how different to former occasions. The islanders, who would not formerly speak to each other, or assemble under the same roof, came together and filled the hall — the servant ran out for more seats...all the islanders were come."

After nine unsuccessful attempts to land on 25th June 1843,

"I determined never again to devote a Sunday to the island of Lundy."

Trinity House tardiness in attending to the enclosure walls brought them into conflict with Heaven's tenant Mr Rowles, who wrote in August of 1844 (THGLA 1844):

"...representing that his crops have received much injury and that he has otherwise been put to great inconvenience and expence by reason of the Cattle trespassing thereon consequent upon the ruinous state of our enclosure walls, which are a part of the fence which separates the Northern and Southern parts of the Island; whereupon he expresses his expectation that the fences will be immediately repaired and that he shall receive pecuniary compensation for the losses he had been continually sustaining during the past five years."

Despite having obtained estimates for wall repairs a few months earlier, Trinity House denied that the walls could have been the cause of injury, but that if Rowles wished to press his claim he should submit particulars of the damage and state the amount required. After further correspondence and the intervention of Mr Heaven on Rowles' behalf, Trinity House offered Rowles £25 instead of the £100 requested, and undertook to continue the repair of the walls. Rowles rejected the £25, and it wasn't until October 1845 that he received the full £100 claim for losses due to the stock having got into the arable land. The walls in this case evidently refer to the paddock enclosure, and work on them was carried out at the end of 1845. The north wall is adjacent to the wall that Heaven built in 1838 across the island from the Trinity House compound to the west wall of the Tillage Field, now known as the Lighthouse Wall. It is interesting to note that Rowles referred to the land beyond this as "the North".

Meanwhile another dispute arose over the garden walls surrounding the lighthouse. In replacing the eastern wall, Trinity House proposed that the wall should be continued in a straight line across the Burial Ground, with a gate for access, instead of building round it. As the Burial Ground was excluded from their lease and was, presumably, consecrated ground, it is not surprising that Heaven refused to agree, particularly as it would have involved disturbance to existing graves. Unfortunately the plan referred to is not found with the documents, and presumably the walls were built as they now stand.

Accommodation on the island was still in short supply and Heaven asked once again for permission to use the agent's cottage, this time to house the guests for his woodcock shooting. This was granted, but it could not have offered the visitors much comfort, as in 1845 it was suggested that it might be pulled down. Heaven tried to buy it, with a piece of land for an enclosure, but Trinity House refused. It was repaired and Heaven was accorded the use of it for a few days at a time when it might be available. At that time the Heaven family was resident on the island every summer, and the year-round population consisted of the tenant farmer Rowles, his family, servants and labourers, and the two lighthouse families.

Monk evidently did not find Lundy, or his superior, tolerable, as after two years he made the first of repeated applications for a transfer. There is evidence of conflict with Phelps, who informed the Committee of Lights inspectors that Monk had given oil away to the workmen (THGLA 1846).

> "The charge is entirely denied by Monk, and by the Foreman of the Works...and the proofs of it are very insufficient. Mr Phelps stated that, by his measurement of the Oil, in which he is very particular, a larger quantity was consumed during several of Monk's watches, when the workmen were there, than usual, and that the Workmen were burning Oil, altho' they brought none with them to the island. Monk says, in answer, that the consumption of Oil will vary with the state of the atmosphere, and the draughts in the Lantern, and that the Workmen obtained their Oil out of the empty Tins, which Mr Phelps allowed them to drain, and which he admitted, after having first drained them himself. The Committee are inclined to think that it has not been the case and if it has, that the quantity was very small. Monk was strongly cautioned to be very careful of his conduct for the future."

Bailey, the Trinity House agent from Milford Haven, reported disagreements between the keepers, and the matter was referred to the Elder Brethren. Phelps appears to have been intelligent and zealous, but not an amiable colleague. He was inventive, and he submitted the model of an improvement to the construction of the Argand Burners and the method of mounting the reflectors, for which Wilkins was ordered to make a prototype. This being approved, an order was given for the manufacture of 25 of the burners. The ventilation of the lantern was a problem, it being Phelps' opinion that since the ventilators in the lantern room had been taken away and Faraday's tubes substituted, there was more moisture on the glass, and that a greater number of lamp glasses were broken in the low light. One year later the problem had still not been resolved (THGLA 1845).

"...A good deal of condensation still takes place, at times, on the Glass of the Lantern, although it is greatly lessened by Mr Faraday's smoke apparatus; this may partly be accounted for by there being no door to shut off the damp air of the Tower, as recommended by Mr Faraday at St Catherine's, and partly perhaps by the Smoke Tube being scarcely sufficient to ventilate a 14 feet Lantern...Mr Faraday should be consulted...a door might be fixed on the stairs below the Watch Room and the Stove should be moved down there, as it occasions much dust in the Lantern."

The Committee of Lights went on to report (*Ibid*) that

"The Tower is very damp inside, and the Light Keepers were directed to brush the mould off with a strong brush, together with as much of the paint as they could, and to keep it clean: a small part, which was lime-whited last year by direction of the Committee, is now in a good state, and it will be best to lime-white the whole of it in future. In the Low Light, the Smoke Tubes have not been fitted. The Committee recommend, that when this is being done, the frame of the Reflectors should be lowered 6 inches, as at present the horizontal bars of the semi-lantern nearly intercept the central rays of both tiers of Reflectors."

A picture emerges of the drudgery of the keepers' lives, tending both the upper and lower lanterns on night watches, carrying the oil, keeping the establishment clean and polished, working on maintenance, whitewashing the tower, writing the journals, cultivating their gardens, and carrying water. Neither is there any evidence of arrangements for relief. The keepers suffered additional hardship when the Trinity steamship *Argus* went into dock for repairs to her boilers that took 22 months. Mr Heaven wrote in January of 1846 that he had to take action to relieve the distress to the keepers and their families, and had obtained all that was necessary by his own boatman. He asked Trinity House to recompense the boatman for his extra work over a period of twenty months. On the positive side, the keepers enjoyed an assured income with a pension and the provision of a furnished house that, they were reminded, was considerably better than they would have had otherwise. They were provided with uniforms, coal, candles and land for cultivation or a compensating allowance. In return, they were required to be sober and industrious, clean in their persons and their linen, and to uphold orderly domestic households.

### Instructions to lightkeepers

1. You are to light the lamps every evening at sun-setting, and keep them constantly burning bright and clear, till sun-rising.

2. In order to ensure the perfect fulfilment of the foregoing article, a perpetual watch is to be maintained throughout the night; and in this respect the principal is to take equal duty with the assistant keeper: he whose watch is about to end, is to trim the lamps and leave them burning, in perfect order, before he quits the lantern and calls the succeeding watch; and he who has the watch at sunrise is then to extinguish the lamps, and commence all necessary preparations for the exhibition of the light at the ensuing sun-set.

3. In order to maintain the greatest degree of light the wicks are to be trimmed every three hours, and especial care taken that their tops are cut exactly even.

4. No bed, sofa, or other article on which to recline, can be permitted either in the lantern or in the apartment under the lantern, known as the watch-room.

5. You are to be careful that the lamps and reflectors, or other lighting apparatus, are cleaned and polished every morning, using for that purpose the polishing powder and leathers provided by the corporation, and no other means; the glazing of the lantern is also to be constantly kept, both internally and externally, in the cleanest possible condition.

6. You are to take especial care that neither lamps, candles, coals, or any other article, be left burning anywhere so as to engender fire.

7. You are to see that none of the oil, stores, goods, or materials be wasted, embezzled, or stolen; and that all economy and good management, consistently with the maintenance of a perfectly good light, be in every respect and at all times observed.

8. If any of the lamps, reflectors or windows are broken, or other damage be done to the lighthouse, through carelessness or negligence of the light-keepers, the repair thereof is to be paid for by the person through whose carelessness or negligence the damage occurred.

9. You are strictly forbidden from causing any outbuildings to be erected, or any alteration of the lighthouse premises, or fences to be made, without having first obtained the sanction of the Board.

10. The principal light-keeper is charged with the custody of the oil and stores of every description; he is therefore to keep an exact account of the quantities thereof received from time to time, and of the deliveries for the necessary purposes of the establishment; also an accurate account of the nightly consumption of oil, on the forms provided for that purpose, and to deliver the same, together with the other accounts for which forms are furnished, to the agent, at the regulated periods for transmission to this house.

11. The principal light-keeper is also to keep a journal of all occurrences and observations, and to be particular in describing all circumstances attending them, and to communicate the same on the form provided for that purpose, once a quarter, or oftener, if necessary.

12. The light-keepers are to exercise a proper discretion in the admission of visitors to view the establishment, conducting themselves with civility to strangers and other persons upon all occasions, and observing that no person is, on any account, to be permitted to inspect the interior of the lantern unattended by one of the light-keepers, and they are held responsible that no damage is thereby occasioned to the lighting apparatus, or disfigurement to any part of the premises.

13. The keepers are to attend a place of worship upon each Sunday in turn, and where the rule shall, by reason of distance, be incompatible with the performance of the lighthouse service, the principal keeper shall, at least once in every Sunday, assemble his own family and his assistants and their families, in his own dwelling or other convenient place, and there read to them throughout the Church service for the day; also a sermon or homily from the volume provided by the corporation for this purpose.

14. The light-keepers, both principal and assistants, are cautioned that their retention or promotion in the service depends upon their strict adherence to the rules laid down for their guidance; and also on the constant habit of cleanliness and good order in their own persons, and the preservation thereof in every part of the lighthouse, lantern, and other premises; and they are enjoined to the invariable exercise of temperance and morality in all their habits and proceedings, so that by their example they may enforce, as far as lies in their power, the observance of the same laudable conduct by their wives and families.

15. The principal light-keeper is held responsible for the execution of the duties of the establishment, and the observance of the foregoing regulations.

16. Four times every day…namely at 3 am, 9 am, three pm, and 9 pm, the height of the mercury in the barometer is to be read off and registered, in inches and hundredths of an inch; the height of the attached thermometer is to be noted in degrees; and that of the thermometer, in open air, in degrees and such fractions of a degree as can be estimated by eye.

(National Archives 1845)

Heaven proposed that Trinity House should again serve the lighthouse by sharing the expense of the boat contract, for which their annual contribution would be £25. The proposal was rejected as the Elder Brethren considered that, despite the period of almost two years where no regular supplies were delivered, they still provided a sufficient service. Heaven persevered however, and renewed his offer to engage a vessel from Clovelly once a week for the summer six months, and fortnightly in winter. Trinity House finally agreed to share the cost, although they thought it unnecessary.

Heaven also reported damage to the foundations of the quay and the quay storehouse, and the Board ordered temporary repairs pending an inspection by the Elder Brethren. In September another landslip occurred which affected over thirty yards of the road, and completely blocked the route from the quay. Mr Rowles offered to remove the fallen mass, put the wall up, and repair the road from the beach to the Castle Road for £10, which was approved, although not until ten months later in May 1847. When frost and heavy rains caused two more serious landslips in 1848, carrying away about half the width of the road with danger of further subsidence, Heaven did not wait on Trinity House deliberations but had it repaired and trusted that the Corporation would recompense him. This it did, as it was bound to do by the agreement for use of the road. The same thing happened again in the winter 1849, once again involving a cliff fall from below the castle which made the road impassable on foot, and dangerous.

# Chapter 4

## A NEW AND BRIGHTER LIGHT: 1845–60

The new and stricter version of *Instructions to Light-keepers* issued in 1845 was evidently to remedy problems that had arisen since the first. And then, following an investigation by the Elder Brethren into disagreements between the light keepers, it was decided that John Phelps should be transferred to the post of Principal Keeper at the newly completed Trevose Head lighthouse. He moved there in the autumn of 1847 and William Welch, from Eddystone, was appointed PK at Lundy. This was not the only change in the island population, as at the end of 1846 Captain Jack Lee succeeded Rowles as tenant and, being a retired seaman, he also agreed to tend on the lighthouse. Keeper Monk renewed his application for a transfer in 1848 as his wife was in poor health, but again without success. Whether Henry Reece was on temporary service is not clear, but in 1849 he asked to be transferred as, however magnificent the light, he was over six feet and too tall for the lantern room.

A light keeper described the wreck of the *Ann,* which happened on 2nd February 1848 (Gosse 1853):

> "A vessel came ashore in a dense fog on the rocks just below the lighthouse. All the crew took to their boat, but were never afterwards heard of. One person alone was saved, a sailor boy, but a passenger on board this craft. The boat had put off without him, but the crew…told him to jump overboard, and they would pick him up. He, however, was afraid to do this as he could not swim…The poor lad remained on the wreck till morning dawned; meanwhile the tide had receded, and had left the vessel high and dry upon the shore. He clambered up the precipice, told his sad tale, and met with hospitality and sympathy."

A few days later the Norwegian brig *Sylphiden* was also lost in fog and a total wreck. The farmer Lee described how all hands had been saved by the islanders, who hauled them up the cliffs by means of ropes. In February 1849 the *Valiant* collided with the *Maid of Errin* in thick rough weather between Lundy and Hartland, and vanished from view with all hands in a matter of minutes. A capsized boat, four oars and a kedge anchor were picked up near Lundy, by which the ship was identified. The master left a wife and five children, the mate his wife and six children. In November of the same year the American ship *Archelaus* sank in Lundy Roads, and her crew of 22 was rescued by three pilots from Pill. Each of them later received a reward of £5, and her cargo of 700 tons of railway line was recovered by divers the following year.

Welch was reported to the Deputy Master and Wardens for having been absent without leave from the 8th to 11th May 1850, and without giving notice to the superintendent, which was a very serious offence. His explanation was that he fetched the tidal pole and bought a greatcoat and other necessities for winter. By what means he might have sought permission or given notice was a question not addressed, but in view of his good character he escaped with a reprimand, and a warning that any repetition of such insubordination would render him subject to the Board's severest displeasure. George Monk tried yet again to secure a removal from Lundy for the benefit of his wife's health, and also asked for promotion, but was curtly informed that many stood in line for promotion before him.

The year 1850 had started badly with two wrecks in the first month. An unidentified barque went down with her four crew in the Roads, and two weeks later one life was lost when the *Thomas Crisp* ran ashore in a gale. The sloop *Louisa* ran aground on the west side in February and was a total loss, soon followed by an unidentified ship, possibly the trawler *Medea*. The *Glenlyon* was in collision with another vessel west of Lundy, when the second vessel was lost. It was only identified when a medicine chest and the logbook were found floating. 1851 began with severe gales, when a schooner and a lugger, both unidentified, were total losses and there was only one survivor. The *Columbine, en route* from Newport to Jamaica, took shelter in the Roads in September, and was found to have four feet of water in the hold. She slipped her cable and lost her anchor, but fortunately was able to proceed to Bristol.

In 1851, Mr Heaven and his family took up permanent residence on the island, the only owner ever known to have done so. He became concerned for the education of the island's children. As well as Monk's two children, aged 2 and 6, there were seven other children of school age on the island who, he said, were growing up in absolute ignorance. Mr Heaven therefore asked Trinity House for permission to use the agent's cottage for a school, which was granted. There were just two rooms, with fireplaces, and Jane Welch (Welch's neice) was the teacher.

A family of eight in Heaven's employ lived at the castle, and the tenant Lee lived at the farmhouse with his wife, six male employees, one of whom had a wife who was dairymaid with a baby. The lighthouse personnel made up one quarter of the total population of 28, not one of whom had been born on the island. The establishment of the squire's household on Lundy would have been a welcome addition to the population. He was a lay reader and provided Sunday services in the hall of his house. The family was able to offer some authority, first aid, counsel and support to the islanders, as well as opportunities for employment. A contract was made for a regular boat service, weekly in summer and fortnightly in winter, which brought supplies, mail, news, and occasional visitors.

The naturalist, Phillip Gosse, spent a week on Lundy in 1852, and he made equally careful observation of the lighthouse as of the plants and birds (Gosse 1853).

"A staircase of stone leads up to the lantern, which is a room fifteen feet in diameter, surrounded by panes of thick plate-glass about two and a half feet square. The light is placed in the centre, within a cage, having an octagonal revolving frame: each of the eight squares, of which it is composed, consists of many large lenses of varying powers, so arranged that the light shall be in the focus of all. In order to accomplish this, the central part of every lens, except the middle one, is cut away; and thus we behold a perfect lens in the centre, surrounded by successively-diminishing segments of larger lenses. Square mirrors are placed above and below, in many rows, at such angles as shall reflect the light upon the surface of the sea. The whole combination of refraction and reflection has the effect of producing a most intense glare, when the eye of the beholder is immediately opposite the centre of any one of the lenses...the light...shines with a strong and vivid glare at Ilfracombe, which is twenty-two miles distant...By means of wheel-work, the motive power of which is a weight-and-chain pulley, like that of a clock, the eight-sided frame revolves around the light, with a uniform motion, performing the complete circle in sixteen minutes. Thus a period of two minutes elapses from one moment of greatest intensity to the next; the interval being occupied by a gradual diminution of the apparent light, till the dimmest point is attained; and then a gradual increase to the brightest. At a great distance there occurs an interval of total obscurity; but this is only because the rays are too feeble to be appreciable so far. Within a circle of a few miles the light never quite disappears.

"The fatality which the lanterns of lighthouses occasion to birds has been often mentioned...Lundy Light, it appears, is responsible for its full share of these casualties. The keepers informed us that sometimes four dozen birds are found in a single morning, either killed or helpless, outside the lantern...They mentioned Blackbirds as habitually flying against the panes...[and] snipes...I did not hear that these involuntary attacks had ever the effect of injuring the plate-glass...So great is the power of the lenses, that when the sun is shining, the keepers are compelled to exercise caution in entering the lantern for the purpose of cleaning the lamps. The concentrated rays would quickly set their clothes on fire, if brought into the focus; blinds are therefore necessary, which are always kept down during sunshine.

"The lamp is a large Argand burner, of four circular wicks, placed concentrically, or surrounding each other, with intervals between. In descending, we were shown into a chamber filled with the large cylindrical glass chimneys to be used for the lamp; here they are kept in store, arranged on shelves round the room. Eighteen dozen, as we were told, was the number that we saw. At the bottom of the edifice there is a second light-chamber facing the sea. Here are placed nine hemispherical reflectors, made of copper, polished and silvered within their concavity. They are set in two rows, four above five, arranged in the arc of a large circle. A lamp is placed in the focal centre of each, the smoke from which is led off by a tube, passing through each reflector to a common chimney behind. This lower light is chiefly of use to ships when near the island. As long as it continues in sight, when approaching the shore, they are safe; but the moment it is shut in by the intermediate summit of the precipice, they are in dangerous proximity to the rocks, and must haul off till they see it again. The fogs, which are so prevalent on this coast in winter, are the most fatal occasion of shipwreck. It is then in vain that the watchful keeper trims the lamp, and in vain the inventions of optical science are employed to magnify the light. The dense and blinding mist absorbs the rays, and intercepts the friendly warning."

The light could not have been as effective as Gosse thought, as inspection visits by Trinity House committees in 1853 resulted in recommendations that it should be improved by replacing the mirrors with zones (crystal faces). It was also observed that the revolving light was not perfectly regular, and it was decided that Professor Faraday should be consulted once more.

Since the volume of shipping in the Bristol Channel was high, the effectiveness of the light was extremely important. Today it is difficult to envisage more than 300 ships coming down the channel at once, or to see Bideford as a very significant port. But in the seventeenth century it had been the third most important port in the kingdom, and in 1852 there were still 26 customs officers in place to supervise trade.

Although Lundy Roads was usually a place of shelter, the danger of winds suddenly veering east was illustrated by the fate of the *Wizard* in January of 1852. She was underway from the Roads when struck by blinding rain and a sudden southeasterly gale, force 10, and was driven ashore at the Cove. The crew was safe, but the wrecked ship was sold where she lay for just £40. That was the only wreck recorded in that year.

When, in 1853, the French *Léocadie* collided with a large brig near Lundy, her crew took to their boat and landed safely on the island near the lighthouse. The loss of the *Ariel* 18 miles to the west of Lundy also in 1853 illustrated the hazard of fire-damp for ships carrying wet coal. A boy had been sent down to the hold and unfortunately he dropped the lighted candle by which he was finding his way. This caused the coal gas to ignite with a heavy explosion. The ship was lost with one of the crew killed, another seriously injured, and the ship's boy afflicted by severe burns. The schooner *Auspicious* heard the explosion and went to the rescue of the seamen (Larn, 1996).

The decision processes to be completed before the necessary improvements could be made to the light in 1853 were complicated, when the control of light dues and of financial expenditure were transferred from Trinity House to the Board of Trade. After 1853 the Corporation received only charitable and private income, and had to obtain Board of Trade authority for its non-charitable expenditure. Another result of this change was that Trinity House minutes were altered in format, and from that date were recorded by reference number providing much less detail than previously.

After a long process of recommendations between committees, consultations with Faraday and Wilkins, Messrs Chance were awarded the contract in May

1856 to supply a new catadioptric revolving apparatus for the Lundy Island Light. At £1495 they had submitted the lowest of the tenders (equivalent to more than £90,000 today). This was to be a holophotal light of the first order to maximise the strength of the beam, and was to incorporate a recently developed French system of revolving vertical lenses. A holophotal apparatus had the advantage of extra reflecting prisms above and below the light source, which corrected the loss of upward and downward rays. A first-order light had a focal length of 920 mm, the second most powerful apparatus it was possible to install.

Holophotal light

Before this improvement was in place, four more wrecks occurred. An emigrants' ship from Wales, the *Joseph F. Votsam*, ran ashore one night in 1855 on the Hen and Chickens rocks at the northwest corner of the island. The islanders knew nothing of this until the ship's boats were rowed ashore. The captain, crew and passengers were seen coming up the road, some barely clothed; one small boy wore nothing but a sunbonnet. They gathered at the back door of the Villa, and the captain greeted the domestics and ladies of the house with "Here you are, ladies! I'm bringing you some possible husbands". Clothes for shipwrecked mariners were kept at the Villa, so something, no matter how bizarre, was found for everyone. On the following day the barque *Avon* struck and sank in the same area, and some part of her cargo of copper was later recovered. In the following year the *Wesleyana* steamship was wrecked, again at the north end of the island. In her case efforts were made by divers to recover her engines, but without success. The SS *Loire* also sank at Lundy in 1856, with her cargo of coal from Cardiff destined for Rouen. The only record for 1857 was of the *Frederick*, abandoned in Lundy Roads on 4th November.

By June 1857 the new apparatus was ready for delivery, but once again there had been landslips and the road was badly damaged. Heaven had already written to Trinity House about this, as well as drawing attention to the dangerous state of the cliff above the landing place, but without result.

Now that it was necessary to carry out repairs before the apparatus could be transported to the lighthouse, Trinity House at last employed contractors to do the necessary work.

Robert Stevenson said (Findlay 1861)

> "A first order lenticular apparatus is one of the most beautiful objects in the world... constructed with the utmost skill and refinement, and involving in its structure some of the highest principles of applied science."

However fine it was, the new revolving apparatus suffered teething troubles (THGLA 1857a).

> "The wrong revolution of the Light was reported by Welch, the Principal Keeper, a fortnight after the machinery had stopped and was for two nights worked by the keepers with lines [i.e. manually] after which it again went; a few days after Chance's Mechanic arrived, who found a smaller wheel was necessary, and for which he wrote to Messrs Chance, and waited three weeks for its return and which arrived more than twice too large (which the man stated was the mistake of the Foreman at Birmingham), the Mechanic immediately took back himself the said wheel, was absent one week, returning at noon the day of my arrival at Lundy. The revolution of the Apparatus has recently been in seven minutes instead of sixteen."

The report also echoes a sour note in that the Board of Trade had enforced the acceptance of Chance's tender, against the Trinity House wish to employ Wilkins (THGLA 1857b).

> "On leaving Lundy to the distance of six miles the light appeared fixed with an occasional flash, it then showed as a Revolving Light which suddenly disappeared at nine miles, although the night was remarkably fine and clear, the Pilot observed it might have been a fog on the island which occasionally occurs. I asked Mr Wilkins what he thought of the Light, who observed he was much disappointed with its brilliancy...The Glass of the Lenses is of a good colour, though not equal to the French, nor is the fitting of the Apparatus so well finished."

Trinity House wrote to the Board of Trade that they had favoured special invitation to Mr Wilkins rather than competitive tender, because of his experience with the new French apparatus. They added that the machinery fitted by Chance Brothers, who had been invited to tender by the Board, was of imperfect construction, which caused it to be unreliable. For almost two months there had been either the risk of misleading the masters of vessels, or the light had to be kept at the right rate of revolution by constant manual labour. However, once it had all been put right, the Lundy light was later seen to be magnificent.

In 1857, after ten years of serving at Lundy, Welch requested an onshore posting as he had previously served nine years on Eddystone Rock. The work on Lundy was arduous; there were two lights to service and maintain, and the task of revolving the light manually would have been exhausting. In addition, the keepers would show visitors around the lighthouse, and from time to time would assist at the scene of wrecks. They were required to paint the lantern room, and it was further proposed that they should carry out the whitewashing of the tower and enclosure walls. Welch explained to the inspectors that (THGLA 1857c):

> "...he is no longer without risk of accident to paint the outside of the Lantern, owing to the giddiness that comes on when on a ladder at so great a height, and that Lewis, the assistant keeper, has never been able to do it, he therefore prays the Board that a regular Painter may be allowed for this work, also as regards the Memoranda from the Board 'that the inside of the Tower and Garden Walls be Whitewashed by the Keepers', he begs respectfully to state that his and his Assistant's time are so fully employed in keeping the Lanterns etc in order, and the dwellings clean, that they could not without neglecting their duty in this respect undertake the extra work..."

A complaint was also made that as there was no firewood on the island, the keepers had great difficulty in making their coal allowance suffice. The above demonstrates that Monk had at last been successful in obtaining a transfer, and had been succeeded by Lewis. It is not surprising that the keepers sought transfers, or that there were disputes with the personnel. In 1854 (Welch and Monk), a keeper was convicted of receiving lodgers (which would appear to have been a long-standing practice in view of the shortage of accommodation on the island) and disagreements between the keepers were noted. Another complaint in 1857 (Welch and Lewis) was of drinking, using abusive language and being absent from duty. In the following year there was a conviction for neglect and quarrelling, and another for neglect in 1860 (Hughes and Lewis).

The old light apparatus was removed and taken to South Bishop. In the meantime, the Trinity Engineer had inspected the cliff at the landing place and recommended the construction of a wall to protect the road. The tenant Lee carried out this work for the sum of £47 10s. The repairs of the road and building up of retaining walls made necessary by landslips were a recurrent problem in which Trinity House was consistently slow to act. They tried several times to force Heaven to share the cost, but he succeeded in holding them to the agreement that had been made in August 1842.

About 1836 Mr Heaven had drawn up a petition for a harbour of refuge to be built at Lundy in which he emphasised the potential benefits to shipping, and the suitability of the island and its resources for the purpose. That was at a time when the island was for sale due to his economic difficulties. Clearly there were also potential benefits to him, either in the vast expanse of trade in victualling that a harbour would occasion, as well as in enticing a purchaser of the island. The question was under investigation by a Commission, since 4680 lives had been lost at sea between 1852 and 1857, and the loss in shipping amounted to £1,500,000. It was stated that the trade of the Bristol Channel represented nearly one-sixth of the shipping and one-tenth of the tonnage of the entire kingdom, and that there had been 187 marine casualties there between 1856–57. After enumerating the advantages that Lundy offered, the Commission decided that "...the depth of water in which the breakwater must be necessarily placed...is so great as not to be thought of...". Lundy could not offer facilities for repairs either (Allington *et al.* 1994).

Between 1842 and April of 1858 there are records of twenty-four wrecks around Lundy, and there were also fifteen others for which records have been lost. Although this would seem to show an increase on the figure for 1829–42, the mid-forties to mid-seventies was a time of great industrial expansion, and the volume, size, and speed of shipping in the Bristol Channel increased. This increase made the efficiency of lighthouses more important, both in terms of light power and being distinguishable from others. Heaven, resident on the island year-round, showed an unusual discernment in being the first to point out the salient problem, and the solution for it which was eventually implemented in 1897 (THGLA 1858a).

> "A letter from W H Heaven dated 9th Instant [April 1858] was read [to the committee], adverting to the recent loss of two vessels on that Island and the narrow escape of two others during this Month, all of which he states were lost or nearly so for want of some warning as to their position, and further stating that the Light on that Island is not of the slightest use to vessels when many dark Nights, because when the Island itself is free from it, the Light stands so high that it is capped by Fog, he therefore suggests that at the North and South extremities of the Island there should be erected two low Light Houses one with an Apparatus for sounding a powerful Bell, and the other with a large Gong or Cannon to be fired when required, the difference of sound giving notice to the Mariner nearest to which end of the Island he may be. The consideration of this suggestion was referred to a Joint Committee of the Deputy Master and Wardens and the Committee for Lights."

The suggestion of two new lighthouses with fog signals fell on deaf ears, understandably, as it came immediately after the magnificent and expensive improvement to the light. But enquiries were set in train to explore the practicalities of a fog signal station. Meanwhile, the wreck register for 1858 recorded that 15 vessels were lost at Lundy in that year, though the records of only two have survived. The schooner *Charles* was wrecked on the west side during a severe gale with the loss of five of her crew of seven and the smack *Trident* was lost in a force nine easterly gale and one of her crew perished.

An urgent investigation was made after the lighthouse was struck by lightning during a severe thunderstorm in June 1858 (THGLA 1858b).

"It appears that the Electric Fluid entered on a level with the flooring of the Low Light, where there is copper plate connected with the Lightning Conductor, tearing a hole where it passed through the oil cloth floor carpet, putting out the Lamp of the Northernmost Reflector, in its passage...It had, at the same time, entered the underground oil cellar under the circular stone stand for the oil tins, chipping its stone edge in several places, tearing and scattering about the oil cloth where it protruded from under them, and passing upward through the vaulted stone roof, making a hole about 3 inches long by a 1/4 inch wide on the under side, at the foot of the Tower stairs, scattering the broken stone over the floor of the lower steps, proving that its passage was upward, breaking one of the inner panes of the double window in the upper part of the Tower, and tearing away two small portions of the wood casing into a closet in the Watch Room, immediately over the broken window pane, after which all trace of it was lost. Lewis Hughes, the Principal Keeper, declares that he felt the Tower shake, though he was in bed in his dwelling..."

Captain Close was sent with an engineer to report, and found that (THGLA 1858c)

"The contact of the Conductor with the metal frame of the Lantern is perfect, and the heavy circular Iron Rail of the Gallery outside is connected by a flat copper bar with the Conductor. But the pedestal that supports the Lens, and the revolving machinery, is in no way connected with it, and the stone in the Lantern and Iron Hand Rail of the uppermost flight of stairs, only very indifferently connected. There is moreover a small copper rod 1/2 inch in diameter fixed to this hand rail, its lower end being let into the first or upper stone step. This may originally have been connected with the frame of the old Lighting Apparatus, but it is not so with the present one, it is now of no use, and may be a cause of the accident...About 10 feet below the Lantern (supported on two heavy iron girders) is an iron platform about 4 feet by 10 feet, on which stood the Revolving Machinery of the old Apparatus (now moved into the Lantern). The Lightning Conductor just touches one of these girders, but as they are four feet apart and deeply let into the wall the contact of the one furthest from the Lantern does not appear sufficient; and the iron hand rail, which terminates here, has no connection with the platform or the Conductor... About ten feet below the iron platform is the first stone floor under the Lantern, the seams of this floor are leaded, and two heavy iron bars about 4 feet long by 4 inches broad are let into the stone floor, they are unconnected with the iron rail to the upper platform, and but indifferently connected with the one leading downward and through it, with the Conductor...on the next floor below where the lightning appears to have run along the lead of one of the seams on which the woodwork partition stands, three explosions have taken place at intervals of six inches tearing away portions of the Wood Work..."

Captain Close found that the earthing was in good order, and he evidently did not support the arresting idea that the current had travelled upwards, so the report was referred to Professor Faraday for his opinion.

The loss of another eight vessels at or near Lundy was recorded during 1859. Of those, seven un-named ships were lost in a single ferocious gale, and four of the victims, whose bodies were washed ashore, were buried on the island. Soon after that the *Diligent* was another casualty.

A visitor to the island around 1860 (Anon, *c.*1860) was very much impressed by the lighthouse:

> "...with its lofty white tower...Everything in it was kept scrupulously clean — not a speck of dust could be seen on the whole of the flight of stone steps leading from the basement to the top lantern room. The condensers and reflectors to the lamps were like masses of polished silver. Nothing appeared to be neglected. On the top of the tower there is a kind of balcony, surrounded with iron railing. I cannot express my peculiar sensations on getting out on this place, and looking down the cliffs, with the sea lashing their base hundreds of feet below...Near and far a hundred sails enliven the Channel. Some, passing up with every inch of white canvas stretched... others shifting and tacking and struggling to make headway."

He had crossed to the island with a former keeper (Welch) who was making a return visit to see Lee, the farmer. The visitor continued

> "It is almost astonishing with what feelings he spoke of revisiting the scene of his former labours."

Later in the day the writer returned to the farmhouse:

> "...the sounds of music struck on my ear, as well as loud bursts of hilarious merriment...the Ranger's crew and the farm labourers were…just getting up an extemporaneous dance in the large roomy kitchen...each person had got a glass containing a white liquid which appeared to me to be milk. But I thought the consumption of that article could not account for the broad grin on the honest visage of my new acquaintance, the farmer. The fine bronzed face of the old lighthouse keeper was radiant with smiles, while the captain of the Ranger was amusing the company by dancing a hornpipe...I had reason to suspect that there were other ingredients besides milk in the glasses...rum, that had never been gauged by the excise men."

The keepers lives were improved by Captains Close and Nisbet who visited to inspect and recommended that new ranges were to be installed, as the old ones were worn out. The assistant keepers were to have a copper in the outhouse at a cost of £1 12*s* 3*d*. It was also ordered that the cesspools and the rainwater cisterns were to be emptied. The following year the keepers were instructed to finish painting the interior of the lighthouse, the gates and the flagstaff, and to whitewash the outhouses and cellars. The PK was also to insert a piece of tubing to the chimney in the lantern, which improved the light very much. It was observed that the lantern door had to be left open, as the only ventilation consisted of the draught up the tower. The captains' visits were routinely made in conjunction with the delivery of annual supplies for the operation of the lighthouse. They cast a keen eye over the whole establishment and made follow-up visits when they felt them to be necessary to maintain good order throughout.

# Chapter 5
## CANNONS IN THE FOG: 1860–73

James Douglass was the Trinity House engineer, a man "immensely respected and popular", who sent his son Nicholas to Lundy to inspect the damage caused by another landslip below the castle, and to arrange for the repair of the retaining wall. Another issue for attention was Heaven's complaint about the state of the walls enclosing the "vacant ground" (the present paddock).

As early as 1859 it was recommended that the Elder Brethren should give consideration to the possibility of planning for a new lighthouse and fog signal system at the north end. But by 1860 measures were underway to place a fog gun on the westernmost point of the island to give warning when the lighthouse was obscured by fog. A site was agreed, for which Heaven asked for £250. Trinity House did not agree to this, but employed an independent surveyor to go to Lundy and make a valuation, which was put at £122 as a one-off payment and which Heaven was forced to accept, with the proviso that the site and buildings would revert to the owner of the island should its use be discontinued. It is not noted what the surveyor's fee and expenses amounted to, but they must have reduced or obliterated the saving on the requested amount.

Work for the new fog signal station, at what later came to be called the Battery, started in 1861 under the direction of Nicholas Douglass, after the Board of Trade had approved estimates of £822 for the construction and £230 10s for the annual running costs. The labourers were housed in the agent's cottage, which had to be re-floored and repaired for them — an indication that the school had not survived the departure of Welch and his family. By June there had been two applicants for the posts of gunners. One of the applicants, Thomas Lee, was a son of the Captain Lee who had farmed the island in the 1850s, and the other was John Blackmore. Both were interviewed, deemed suitable, and appointed with Lee as the principal, with the draconian rider (THGLA 1862a):

> "… that it being clearly understood that the services of these men will be required only so long as Fog Guns shall be maintained, at the respective stations, and that they shall not be entitled to receive superannuation allowance or claim to become subscribers to the Insurance Scheme…[and are] on probation for Six Months."

The Fog Signal Station from the north (Heaven archive)

Meanwhile, a new principal keeper had been appointed at the lighthouse. Wallace was described as a very intelligent man, who evidently brought the lighthouse into spanking order. However, there were still problems of ventilation in both the upper and lower lights, and the keeper stated that he had painted the lower room seven times within the year, but that the room still looked dirty from smoke. The stands for the oil cisterns had to be replaced, and Douglass was authorised to carry out various repairs, including a "pillow to support the floor of the Lantern...when the old lantern was taken away the large hole that the shaft went through was never properly filled up". Douglass was able to improve the ventilation in the low light, and Messrs Chance were called in to make adjustments and repairs to the upper light. The committee could not avoid noting on their journey coming across from Caldey that the light was hidden by fog, and when they were at the lantern room in the lighthouse the fog was rolling around them, while conditions were quite clear at sea level.

The Parliamentary Report on Lighthouses was published in 1861 and gave many details of the nature and running of the two lights as they were found when visited by the commissioners aboard the *Vivid* in 1860. They landed in darkness, found the path up to the plateau very steep and the birds very noisy. The lighthouse was in first-rate order, with the light reflectors well polished, and every part of the establishment a model of cleanliness. It was remarked that the metal fittings were painted, which was considered to be of advantage as opposed to polishing, since the danger of injuring the angles of the prisms or of damaging the lens with polish were avoided, and the extra labour of polishing gave no advantage. The PK remarked that the lens light in the lantern was not half the trouble of a reflecting light of equal power. Overall, the verdict of the commissioners was that the Lundy light ranked first amongst all the lights mentioned, either at home or abroad.

The need for augmentation of warning during fog was highlighted by the wreck in June 1861 of the *Valentine* on the west coast, in dense fog, near the lighthouse. Before the vessel drifted onto the rocks and became a complete loss the crew was able to take to the boats and no life was lost, but it was wryly remarked that had the guns been in place, the accident would not have happened. Nothing could have saved the *Lewis Charles,* which had sunk earlier in the year after a collision with the *Bottreux Castle* during an easterly gale. The *Alert* also sank in October and was a total loss. The last wreck in 1861 was the *Ranger*, which came to grief in the Roads and was left bottom-up with a large amount of wreck floating around. Only one sunken vessel is recorded for 1862, the *Ben McCree*.

The story of the loss of the *James* in March 1862 is harrowing: she sprang a leak off Mumbles in a freshening easterly wind, and by the time she was fifteen miles from Lundy she began to sink and her crew took to their boat. They intended to make for Ilfracombe, but the force of the wind was too great, so they made for Lundy and laid to until daylight. They then made towards the landing beach, obviously ignorant of the treacherous nature of an easterly-driven sea. There, the boat capsized, and only one man survived to land. The bodies of the captain, the mate, and two of the crew were buried on the island.

There would have been fewer pilots at Lundy after 1861, when pilotage for vessels to Cardiff, Newport or Gloucester was no longer compulsory, and they withdrew altogether after 1891 when pilotage for Bristol was required only within the limits of the port. Although they had been of service in carrying letters and in some other ways, especially before the Heaven ownership, and had been customers at the stores, they were suspected of stealing birds' eggs, and of collusion in illicit trading in smuggled and stolen goods.

**Information gathered by the commissioners visiting in 1860:**

THE UPPER LIGHT

The height of the tower from base to vane is 96 ft, and a lightning conductor is provided.

The light is a dioptic apparatus of the 1ˢᵗ order. There are 8 refractors or polyzonal lenses of 8 to the circle, with 24 zones of prisms, 18 above and 6 below the lenses, fountain, a 4 concentric wick lamp, with regulating conductor. Clockwork revolving machine. A perfect revolution is made every 16 minutes, showing a flash every two minutes. In 1857 the present apparatus was substituted for the dioptric apparatus with mirrors. The ventilation is by Faraday's tube, 4½ ins in diameter, over the lamp.

The dimensions of the lamp room are: diameter 14 ft height: of pedestal 4 ft 6 ins, of glass 10 ft, of glass to vane 13 ft 6 ins, total 28 ft. The cost in 1843, including the fitting of new apparatus, was £1902 18s 4d.

The distance of the sea horizon from the light is 24¾ miles, and the light can be seen for 32 miles with the naked eye in clear weather. The horizontal range is 360°.

The average annual cost of repairs, since construction, including the low light, is £71. 12s 6d. The average annual cost of painting (every 4 years) is £19 14s. There are two keepers, one paid £65 annually, and the other £46 10s plus one suit of clothes annually, coal, oil, and furniture for the dwellings. In 1857 421 gallons of oil was used and 3 yards of wick; in 1858 435 gallons of oil and 33 yards of wick at 7½d per yard. I gallon of oil burns for 10.069 hours. The total income from the light in 1852 had been £1795 12s 3½d; expenditure had been £362 1s 5d.

The oil is stored in a vault below the ground floor of the tower, of which the diameter is 17 ft 7½ ins, and the height 7 ft 5½ ins.

There are no arrangements for the relief of the keepers.

General repairs cost £496 19s 9d in 1852, and £532 5s 9d in 1858.

THE LOWER LIGHT

There is a fixed, bright catoptric light. Argand lamps have 9 burners of ⅞ of an inch, and parabolic reflectors 21 ins in diameter and 9 ins deep, arranged in two tiers concavely against the wall of the tower. Ventilation is provided by Faraday's tubes of 1¼ ins over the flames of the lamps. In 1857 287 gallons of oil and 58 dozen wicks were used, and in 1858 332 gallons of oil and 45 dozen wicks. The wicks were made of Argand cotton which cost 2s 6d per gross. The dimensions of the light room are: length 11 ft 6 ins, width 6 ft 6 ins, height of glass 4 ft 5 ins. The cost was £2049 18s.

(National Archives 1861)

Strangely, there is no remark made or date recorded for the inauguration of the Fog Signal Station, though it apparently took place in June 1862. A series of whitewashed stones marked the path from the lighthouse, and a steep path led down the cliff side to two cottages, facing north. The two gunners lived there with their families and were provided with a stone reservoir and a well sunk in the small open space outside the cottages. This was a very confined space for two families with children, and although 10s per man was allocated for renting garden space from Heaven, the Corporation refused to enclose it and the allowance was increased to 20s per year in lieu. Beyond the cottages were steps down to a row of three small outbuildings for two privies and an ammunition store, from where a further flight led down to the gun platform and gun-house, facing west. Although the cottages are now in ruins, the entire Battery complex is still there and can be visited in safety.

The Battery outhouses: an ammunition store and latrines

The guns were two eighteen-pounder iron cannons, fired with a charge of three pounds of powder every ten minutes during fog, which could sometimes last for days. The interval of firing was determined by the minimum time it took to clean and reload the gun. The guns remain on site, and carry the royal crest with the cipher GR 1838. The gun-house had a corrugated iron roof, held by iron stays, so that it would blow off in case of an explosion and dissipate the force of the blast. The gun in use was placed in the grooves in the centre of the gun-house, with the muzzle projecting through the window.

In the first year of use the fog gun was fired 788 times, and once prevented the loss of a ship that was sailing immediately below it. But the gunners were issued with an injunction not to fire the gun unnecessarily. This was not taken too seriously, as demonstrated by an account of a pleasure excursion two months later which described how the gun was fired in honour of the visitors. It was found necessary to increase the stock of gunpowder; half was kept at the quay storehouse, presumably to minimise any risk.

The boatman Bragg was contracted by Heaven to run a skiff service from Clovelly weekly in summer, and fortnightly in winter, the expense of which was divided with Trinity House at £25 each per annum. Since Bragg had carried out extra services during the construction of the fog station, he was given an *ex-gratia* payment of £25 by Trinity House, and it was also agreed that he should have another £5 per annum in respect of the extra service that would be required on a regular basis (although the boatman had asked for £25, and Heaven had recommended £15).

The establishment of the fog signal station brought the number of Trinity House families living on Lundy to four. The 1861 census gave only summary figures of the population, but by 1871 (when the number of Corporation families was five) the lighthouse and gun station personnel represented 28 out of a total population of 65, of which 29 were children. The population had been hugely augmented in 1863–64 as Mr Heaven had granted the lease of the island to a company for the exploitation of the granite. The Lundy Granite Company took over the whole island, with the exception of the portion at the southeast reserved for the Heaven family and the Trinity House sites.

The manager of the granite company, who asked Trinity House for the use of the agent's cottage until they were able to build, highlighted the problem of the limited accommodation on Lundy. Use of the cottage was granted at a nominal rent of 1s per month, on the terms that it was not for use by labourers and should be restored to perfect condition on vacation. This was modified to returning it to its original condition, but permission to build an extension was refused. The arrival of the granite company brought great changes to the hitherto quiet and isolated island. The island population rose to more than 200, a store, refreshment room and bakery were built, and a quay and jetty were constructed on the east side. A school, a mission room, a hospital and clinic were established, and there was — for the first time ever — a resident doctor. Quarrying operations were carried out along the east sidings, new buildings were put up north of Quarter Wall and in the village, and north and south wings were added to the farmhouse. The face of Lundy and life for the inhabitants were changed and the accommodation problem resolved, but quarrying came to an abrupt end in 1868 when the company suddenly went into liquidation. It took another four years for the legal complications to be resolved before Mr Heaven was once more in full possession of his island.

Meanwhile, an intriguing wreck on the east side in 1864 was that of the paddle steamer, *Iona II*. The circumstances were questionable, and one of the crew suspected that it was an insurance claim (Dixon 1973). He wrote

"This eighteen-knot steamer set off in fine style for Charleston with two train-loads of armaments...He was set to steer...and not relieved for several hours. Then the pilot came aft alone and told him he would be relieved in half an hour. The ship continued to go ahead at full speed, and no officer had been near him to check the course steered, although there was some fog about. At last relief came, and Henry went forward to his bunk. He had just reached it when the ship went full tilt on the rocks of Lundy Island, tearing out the bow frames and plates as though they had been cardboard."

It appears that before leaving the Clyde the *Iona* was greatly strengthened, and the elegant saloon cabin removed from the deck, so as to make her fit for her passage from Queenstown to Nassau, for which place she was bound. Not being aware of Admiral Fitzroy's storm signal, Captain Chapman put to sea on Saturday last about 1 o'clock, and soon after the vessel encountered a severe gale from the south-west, with a heavy head sea. After facing the storm to a distance of about 170 miles, the captain made for Lundy Island, in the Bristol Channel, in the hope of getting into Milford-haven. On getting to the leeward of the island it was found that the water had increased so rapidly that the fires were put out and the engines brought to a stand. Every exertion was made by the captain and crew to save the vessel; all worked harmoniously together, but, unfortunately, without effect. The firemen even stood up to their middle in the water throwing coals into the furnaces so long as the fires burned, but the pumps soon became choked, and the fires were then put out. The Bristol pilot boat No. 32, Captain Alfred Ray, bore down to the steamer and lay by her until the whole of the crew, 39 in number were safely conveyed on board in the boats of the *Iona*. The water was up to the cabin table the last time the captain went down, and half an hour after the crew left her the steamer sank. The captain of a little schooner offered to stand by the steamer, but the wind blew her off, and the generous seaman had not the opportunity of rendering the assistance he desired.

(The Times 1864a)

The store and refreshment room
(Wide World, July 1906)

*Iona II* (courtesy of Valerie Fenwick)

At her setting out the ship was said to have been a blockade-runner for the South in the American Civil War. The wreck was identified in 1973, and it is now protected under the Protection of Wrecks Act, 1973. There was another casualty due to fog, the steamship *Matilda*, which struck at the northeast corner of the island in 1864. In October of that year the *Superior* was involved in a collision with an un-named vessel, and was sunk. This pinpoints the continued problem of fog warnings, since the cannons placed low-down on the west side were not heard on the east. The *Hector* was another that struck the island in fog in 1865, but the damage was not fatal and later she was refloated and taken to Cardiff for repairs. The only other ship lost in that year was the *Eclipse*, which was stranded.

The Heaven family at Benjamin's Chair, 1864, L to R: W H Heaven, unknown,
Revd H Heaven, unknown, Miss Cecilia Heaven, De Boniot Spencer Heaven,
Mrs Spencer Heaven, Miss Amelia Heaven (Heaven archive)

Cardiff. The captain and crew of the splendid new steamer *Matilda*, of
Glasgow, arrived at this port, having been taken off Lundy Island, where their
steamer had been wrecked. The *Matilda* left Cardiff on Monday afternoon,
with a cargo of steel, iron, and coal, which was reported to be intended for
the Confederates, and is said to have been reported by the American Consul
to his Government. The steamer was built at Glasgow, at a cost of nearly
£60,000, and her trial trip had been made from that port to Cardiff. She
left here on Monday afternoon…and proceeded down Channel, and about
11 o'clock the same night, the captain states, she struck upon Lundy Island,
a thick fog being prevalent at the time, and the ship's compass eight degrees
out. The crew only escaped with a few things, and the vessel now lies many
feet under water. Among the persons who were on board…is a major
Pearson, who states that he belongs to the Confederate artillery.

(The Times 1864b)

By comparison, there are records of occasional pleasure steamer excursions, and the light keepers and gunners would seem to have been hospitable. Voyagers from the *Prince of Wales* in August of 1868 landed on a foggy day, and found the lighthouse to be hardly visible until they were almost upon it. But then, since the ladies of the party were tired (North Devon Journal 1868):

> "...the wife of one of the officials of the lighthouse very kindly provided them with refreshment, and the officials were most kind and polite in explaining the different objects in the tower...The lamps and reflectors are kept beautifully polished, and, indeed, every object bore signs of the greatest order and cleanliness...We made the circle of 147 steps to the top of the tower, in which was placed the revolving lantern, which was rather a leg-aching bit of business; but the nerves of my fair friends would not allow them to go outside, the protection being a single small band of iron running round the tower...[We] made our way to the signal gun battery...the pathway being marked with short pillars of granite...One of the keepers was ill, but the other had been constantly at work during the fog, firing the gun. There were...two eighteen pounders (one only, however, is used, the other being reserved in case of accident). During fine clear weather the officials amuse themselves by shooting the sea birds or gathering their eggs in the crevices of the rocks. We were shown some beautiful specimens killed and stuffed on the island."

Contractors painted the lighthouse establishment throughout every four years, and the Fog Signal Station was whitewashed as well, including the guiding wall down from the plateau. Trinity House heavy supplies were delivered annually, usually in April–June. Periodic visits of inspection were made by officers of the Corporation, which were recorded in the Lighthouse Order Book (Appendix 4). The surviving Order Book dated from 1854, and showed that extra visits were made as and when necessary to investigate mishaps or complaints. Apart from ensuring that the light was properly maintained and the establishment in good order, some interesting additional information can often be gleaned. For example, on 21st July 1862, it was noted that the masonry of the Gun House had been damaged by the firing of the cannon, and the gun establishment required (THGLA 1862b):

> "White lead and boiled oil, Printed instructions for Gunmen, A Hand-spike – Barometer and Thermometer, An Order Book and Box of library ditto, Bell for each cottage, Medicine chest – Tin letter box."

The inevitable road repairs were carried out at intervals, and repairs and minor alterations were carried out to the light from time to time, particularly to improve the ventilation. The keepers reported that they had to leave the lantern room door open, even in winter, and that the lower light room was constantly blackened by smoke.

In 1864 the visiting committee recommended the appointment of a second assistant light keeper, but the Board of Trade was not in agreement, and questioned how one more keeper would enable the organisation of watches providing for one keeper each for the upper and lower lights. The Trinity House argument was that it would shorten the duration of the watches, so that at each relief the keeper in turn for duty would be able to attend efficiently to the lower light before relieving the keeper in the upper light, by which arrangement the instructions never to leave the overflow lamp could be rigidly enforced.

At length approval was given, and in March 1866 the Board sanctioned the expenditure of £500 for a cottage for the PK to be built in the lighthouse compound, and a further £100 for the garden walls. A small outhouse was also built at the northeast corner of the compound for the use of the keeper living in the new house, which provided for an earth closet, and housing for a pig. A pig was an important part of household economy. It could be fed on household and farm waste, its meat could be preserved for winter food (every part of the carcass could be used) and, contrary to modern perceptions, it is by nature a clean animal. From the reports before the extra keeper was decided upon it is clear that the keepers' wives and families were regarded as auxiliaries by the Board, without appointment or status, and unpaid. The keepers and gunners were also expected to double up for each other in case of illness or when a rare leave of absence had been granted.

The gun house at the Fog Signal Station, 1920. The tie rods would have enabled the roof to lift off in the event of an explosion (photo courtesy of Lundy Field Society)

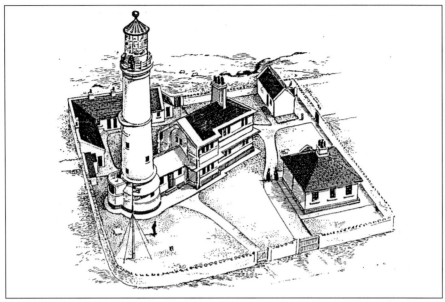

Drawing of a model of the lighthouse compound, made in 1893 (courtesy of John Dyke)

Gunner Blackmore was in poor health, but he had been able to take advantage of the services of the granite company physician, Dr Lineker, in 1865. However, he was charged excessively, and Trinity House was rather less than generous in meeting the bill for £10 10s. Blackmore had to pay £4 4s of it, which for him was the equivalent of three weeks' pay (now £273). Dr Lineker then proposed that he would tend the light-keepers and gunners for £10 10s per year, and the wives and families for a further £10 10s, but was curtly informed that was far more than was paid at other stations. Dr Lineker lived with his sister and niece in the south of the three houses now referred to as Quarter Wall Cottages. He was said to have gone to Lundy to overcome an addiction to drink — a goal he was apparently unsuccessful in achieving.

The third lightkeeper appointed in 1866 was Joseph Bennett, who was accompanied to Lundy by his wife, Jessie.

> Mrs Bennett was fortunate that at that time when her baby was born there was a resident doctor on the island in the service of the Lundy Granite Company. The baby was christened Joseph by the Revd Hudson Heaven on 26 May. As there was no church on Lundy at that time the ceremony would have been carried out in the "Iron Room," a community room for the granite company employees, which stood on the site of the present sheep dip.
>
> (Illustrated Lundy News 1973)

The islanders were witness to the heart-rending loss of the *Hannah More* on 10th January 1866. She was a full-rigged sailing ship bound from Callao to Queenstown, laden with guano, anchored for shelter in the Roads. During the night she was hit by a force nine easterly gale, and a newspaper report described the fearful effect of it (THGLA 1866):

> "It was at first thought advisable to slip anchors and run to sea, but as on the first attempt to set sail the canvas was blown to minute fragments, this was seen to be impossible, and dismay was caused by finding that the ship was dragging her anchors…the cable of one anchor parted, and the ship swung round, exposing her broadside to the fury of a heavy cross sea. Almost instantly her decks were swept clean of every article not firmly fixed, and even a portion of her bulwarks was torn away, her boats and topsails also going by the board. Came the first gleam of morning, and the inhabitants of the island crowded to the cliffs, but speedily saw that the fate of the *Hannah More* was sealed. The crew were seen to be tenaciously, as for very life, clinging to the rigging, helpless and exhausted…It was resolved to attempt a rescue."

By that time the stricken ship was less than five hundred yards off the beach to the south of the landing place, known as Hell's Gates, which could only be reached at high tide by climbing over the steep promontory of Lamatry. By a tremendous effort the islanders managed to manhandle a boat across, and then two men attempted to row it out to the wreck. The raging sea beat them back, despite their heroic efforts, and a second attempt was no more successful.

> "The effort was then seen to be hopeless. And then occurred an incident which made the blood of the spectators boil with indignation…A screw steamer hove into sight and came near the shore…Presently steam was again put on and…the steamer proceeded on her course…Within a few minutes…a giant wave lifted the shattered hull and dashed it with tremendous force against Rat Island. A loud crash was heard above the roar of the waves."

The small boat put out once again, and

> "by a stupendous effort were successful in bringing off five men, who were landed on the beach and pulled up the cliffs by the rope. Before the boat could be got afloat again the ship had broken up."

One man had managed to swim far enough to grasp a rope thrown to him, and was pulled up the cliff. Two others attempted to swim in, but were overcome, and the remainder of the crew were seen to drift westwards clinging to pieces of the wreckage. The islanders recovered one body for burial, and cared for the six survivors for several days until they could be taken to Clovelly. 19 of the crew of 25 were lost. A schooner, the *Olive Branch*, was the only other ship recorded as having sunk in that year.

The Royal National Lifeboat Institution granted awards to the crews of lifeboats "for their gallant services in saving the crews of wrecked vessels during the recent gales".

Six pounds were awarded in respect of the *Hannah More*.

(The Times 1866)

The ship which passed by the wreck could not have been the *Flora* …The Bristol pilot who boarded the *Hannah More* stated that he tried to get the captain to proceed higher up the Channel for shelter, but the master insisted that the pilot went to 'Combe for orders. As there was no telegraph at 'Combe, he had to travel on to Barnstaple. It was this delay which largely contribute to his being unable to return to the *Hannah More*.

Michael Bouquet, 3 January 1964, letter to John Dyke

In 1867 the sailing ship *Columba* of Genoa ran ashore in fog and was stranded on the beach. Fortunately, one of Mr Heaven's daughters was able to speak Italian, and the captain said that the ship had a leak and the crew had been shifting the cargo to be able to make a repair at low tide. This seemed to explain Mr Heaven's puzzlement as to why a ship had run on to the beach in daylight and fair conditions, but later the unruly crew presented themselves at the Villa, knocking loudly on the back door because the ship was alight. It was a wreck, and it provided the islanders with timbers that lasted a long time. It was noted also that it had been heavily insured. The wreck had an unfortunate consequence when one of the islanders was dismantling the rigging; the mast fell on him and he was killed, leaving a widow with small children not provided for. Also in 1867 Tom Lee was granted permission to receive a gratuity of £2 2*s* for assistance given to the master of a vessel called the *Firefly* when it was stranded on Lundy, but that is all that is known about that case.

Twelve ships were wrecked near or ran ashore Lundy in the five years following the establishment of the Fog Signal Station, and concern about the loss of lives and vessels prompted the Reverend Hudson Heaven (eldest son of the island owner) to write to the Board of Trade in 1867. He cited two causes of the inefficiency of the lighthouse: its great elevation, and the long intervals between the firing of the fog signal guns. Trinity House replied that the elevation of the lighthouse had often been under consideration, but the need to carry out more urgent works had meant that the money had to be spent elsewhere than on rebuilding the light at Lundy. They added that it was proposed to establish a Light on Hartland Point.

Meanwhile Douglass supervised general repairs to the lighthouse at a cost of £540, and he reported that the new dwelling would cost £100 more than estimated because of the very wet and stormy weather that had affected building work. Another problem was that the vibration of the lantern had caused eight panes of glass to crack. The remedy was to increase the thickness of the panes from five-sixteenths to half an inch, and to keep a reserve store of twelve panes, but Board of Trade sanction for the expenditure had to be obtained first.

Visits to Lundy and Hartland and a series of committee meetings resulted in a recommendation in August 1868 that (THGLA 1868a)

> "A new Light House to exhibit a Revolving Light be erected on the North End of Lundy island and that the Light shewn from the Lower part of the Tower of the present Light House be discontinued thereat."

However, the examining committee argued that with a North End light-house (THGLA 1868b)

> "...there will be no guide to the important anchorage under Lundy and there would be a necessity for a light on the S.E.point...The Committee consider that the placing of two first-class lights within two and a half miles of each other so objectionable that they recommend to the Court to retain the high light on Lundy but to extinguish the fixed light in the lower part of the Tower and to show a revolving light similar to the high Lundy Light, from the Fog Gun Station when the Light is obscured in haze. On reference to the Logs it will be seen that fog is noted 194 times on 481/2 days at the High Light House during the year 1867, and the signal gun was fired 1,554 times...These figures will give 13 per cent for the duration of Fog and 4 per cent for the firing of the gun. So that it may be estimated that the obscuration of Lundy Light by Fog amounts to about one night in 50."

The matter continued to pass between committees for another three years until in January of 1871 the Board of Trade was informed that (THGLA 1868–71)

> "...as any change on Lundy must be affected by the pecuniary question and also by its relation to the lighting of adjacent headlands we do not regard it as expedient to go more closely into the matter at present."

With that, the question was relegated to the files, but a lighthouse was built at Hartland Point by 1874.

In the meantime, AK Gilpin's wife was very ill during July 1868, and the doctor recommended their removal from Lundy before the winter came. Another committee was sent in 1869 to investigate a complaint against AK Griffiths, who found that he was not fit for the service, and recommended that he should be removed immediately. The same committee was both astonished and very displeased to find eight children living at the Fog Signal Station where, in their opinion, there should not be any. Probably the gunners had been taken by surprise, as the Heaven family log commented that when the Trinity House yacht was sighted, the children were made to run up the sideland behind the Battery and hide until the officers had departed for the beach.

A Lundy Granite Company shipment of granite by the *Caroline* from the quarries to their depot at Fremington left their jetty in the evening of 2nd February 1868 and anchored for the night in the Roads. She begun to leak, and when the wind swung round to the northeast the pumps could not deal with the amount of water, and it was thought best to run her aground on the beach, which was done. Six of the islanders got a rope to her, and were able to bring the crew safely to land. By the end of the month the ship was a partial loss, with the cargo discharged, which may well account for the granite boulders now lying piled at the north end of the beach.

During 1868 no fewer than seven ships were lost on or near the island of which the *East Anglian* was the first. The schooner *Trelissick* sank and was a total loss, the sailing barque *Admiral* sank in a force nine gale that veered from southeast to southwest, and the *Swift* was abandoned by her crew when anchored near Lundy as they were unable to pump the inrush of water any longer. They did not land on Lundy, but were able to get to Clovelly in their own boat. The schooner *Julia* was sheltering in the Roads, but sank there, also thought to have been because of a leak, and of the sailing smack *William* there is only the information that she sank with a cargo of gravel.

Measures were taken to try to limit the widespread plunder of wrecks and, at the request of the Board of Trade, extraordinary permission was given for PK Howgego to act as deputy receiver of wreck for Lundy (Barnstaple district). This was given on condition that his appointment did not interfere with carrying out his normal duties. One (cf. pg. 73) recorded occasion of his acting in case of a wreck is at the loss of the *Brenda* just north of Brazen Ward in 1871, but there were several other wrecks following his appointment at the end of 1867. Wrecking (that is, illegal stripping of goods from a wreck) took place regularly for many years both before and afterwards. As the Heaven family lamented in their diary, it was difficult to prevent in an isolated spot. Howgego was removed from Lundy in 1874.

After the collapse of the granite company in the autumn of 1868 the island store was maintained, but there was no longer a doctor or a school. The Reverend Heaven was concerned about the latter and asked Trinity House for assistance in providing one. This was not an unreasonable request since by 1871 eight of the fifteen children of school age lived at the lighthouse or the fog signal station, and the Education Act of 1870 instituted elementary education for all. Mr Heaven offered to provide a schoolroom and a cottage for a school-mistress, and to pay £10 of her salary of £26 per year. No further references have been found to a school, and the Heaven archives make no mention of a schoolmistress, so the application must have been unsuccessful. Indeed, the Heaven family themselves provided the children with some education.

The sorry catalogue of shipping loss continued during 1869. The brig *Herminia* sank after a collision to the north of Lundy. The pilot cutter *Albion* with a crew of three was cruising the channel seeking a boat requiring pilotage, and anchored in the Roads. When an easterly wind sprang up the only course open to save their lives was to run for the shore, which they did, and when she struck, two fishermen hauled the men to safety through the breakers. The brig *Belinda* was sailing in fog with a valuable cargo of copper when the fog signal gun was heard, and they sighted Lundy. It was not possible to change course quickly enough, and she struck near Black Rock, ran ashore below the cliffs and sank, though her crew was taken aboard the smack *Arbo* and fifteen tons of the copper were later salvaged. This was a case when the point about the interval (ten minutes) between the gunshots being too long was germane. The sailing brig *Margaret* sprang a leak sailing down-channel, and when Lundy came in sight the crew refused to continue pumping in a freshening wind and rough sea. The boats were lowered and the men waited until the vessel sank, but what happened to them is not recorded. Nothing is known of the smack *Eliza* other than that she sank at the end of December and was a total loss.

A problem for the Board of Trade following the exodus of the granite company was in making arrangements for the life-saving apparatus, and Trinity House was asked to allow it to be put in the charge of its personnel. Their reply was that they saw no objection, except that (THGLA 1871)

> "...it is a standing rule with us not to impose any day-work on the keepers which might tend to interfere with their efficiency at night...their duties would be confined to seeing that the apparatus is properly housed and kept up, and that the gear is never used for any purpose other than that for which it is supplied, and that he [the light keeper] should keep the keys of the storehouse."

As the apparatus was removed in 1871 this attempt at an agreement is assumed to have failed.

AK Chavener and his wife had six children, who lost their clothes when a cupboard caught fire in their dwelling. Apart from the question of money, it was wryly observed that there would be no chance of shopping for some time, but the squire and his family helped out as best they could. Another misadventure befell when one of the boys broke his thigh, but there is no description of how this was dealt with. The eldest daughter, Polly, was sent off to the mainland to work at the age of 15.

Nothing had been done about the children at the fog signal station, but when the Trinity House Committee to the Bristol Channel arrived with the annual supplies in July 1873 the number of children there had risen even further (THGLA 1873).

"Landed stores and visited the Establishments, the lighthouse and dwelling clean and in good order, but the Gun Station indifferently clean and to use expressive language disgracefully crowded, there being ten children, two keepers and their wives having only two sleeping rooms, and the place altogether totally unfitted for any children. Lee, the principal, is laid up with rheumatism from which we understood he suffers about nine months of the year, Mr Evans [the shore-based superintendent] informing us that he had not been on the top of the island for months. The committee strongly recommend that a change should be made forthwith."

Twelve days later the superintendent was required to take a doctor with him to the island to issue a certificate as to Lee's health (*Ibid*), and

"to require Blackmore to remove some of his family, there being too many in the dwelling. Lee's family to remain until further instructions."

View north from the Battery cottages (Heaven archive)

Lee, who was lame, had married Anne Withycombe, an islander, in 1864 when she was 21 and he 43; allegedly he secured her hand by promising her a silk gown. They had three children — Annie, Lucy and William — who were all born on Lundy. Blackmore was transferred to the lighthouse service, and Lee was pensioned off in 1873 when the family went to Ilfracombe where he died in 1885. Both were known to be "great poachers", and had their guns confiscated by the Heaven family. When Blackmore's was to be returned to him on leaving, it was found that the case held a carefully wrapped broomstick. It appeared that they had traded in eggs and peat as well as shooting birds and rabbits.

# Chapter 6

## THE FULL ESTABLISHMENT: 1870–84

The total number of wrecks between 1870 and 1873 was fourteen. When the schooner *Thomas Varcoe* sank in the Roads, the crew of six was taken off by Bristol pilot boat number 4 and landed at Ilfracombe. The brig *Mary*, carrying coal, struck between Surf Point and Mouse Island in bad weather and was soon a total wreck. In the Heaven diary it is noted that the crew was rescued by a pilot boat, and that the wrecking by islanders and the pilots went on for four days. The diary also refers to the reported loss of the *John Brogden,* but nothing further is written about it. The *Brenda*, which was a full-rigged sailing ship, ran in to the Knoll Pins on the east side, and a passing tug took off the crew and helped to salvage some of the cargo. Mr Howgego then held an auction of some of the ship's goods on the quay. Salvage operations continued for some time to bring up the cargo of railway iron and the ship was eventually raised, when she had an adventurous passage to Bideford. Early in 1872 the fore-and-after *Mary* was lost. She had been under contract to Mr Heaven since the previous year and fortunately her crew was saved, though the loss of the mail and freight was lamented. When the *Ostrich* came into the Bay for shelter she had the misfortune to collide with the *Betsy*, and sank within five minutes. The *Betsy* went off for repair with the crew from the wreck. Nothing more is known of the *New House,* the *Gertrude* or an unidentified schooner than that they sank at Lundy. The brig *Eliza* sank after a collision with SS *Sir Bevis* at the Rattles and two of her crew, who were lucky to survive, floated on a hatch-cover almost as far as St Ives before they were rescued. A pilot skiff, number 34, was also lost in 1873, and the Heaven diary records on 12th May that "…fishermen saved a barque that was onshore at Gannets Combe".

In 1871 the boatman, Bragg, gave notice that he would not renew his contract, an event which serves to illustrate the cumbersome process of Trinity House decision-making, now further complicated by the need to obtain sanction from the Board of Trade. For some reason the Trinity House committee recommended that a boat should be engaged from Bideford instead of Clovelly, but a *pro-tem* arrangement was made with Bragg for a quarter's service from Clovelly at the rate of £35 per annum. They appeared to have forgotten the contract with Heaven, and at the end of the quarter Heaven protested that since no notice had been given, he had an arrangement in place for the next six months. Trinity House was bound to accept their responsibility in this service, but at the same time gave notice to end the contract. It was clear that Bragg was, reasonably enough, seeking improved terms above the £50 per year that had been agreed in 1847. After the loss of the *Mary* Captain Fishwick replaced her by the *Chase* which Captain Dark of Instow, who had first been employed at Lundy by the granite company, eventually took over.

Bideford was a much larger town, not so remote or steep on the landward side as Clovelly, and had a good quay. However, there was the disadvantage of the Bar at the mouth of the Torridge, which meant that sailing times were limited to high tide. This probably accounts for Trinity House's subsequent change of mind that a tender should not come from Bideford. But Heaven's next proposal was for a steamer service from Appledore at £140 per year, which would have had the same disadvantage of having to navigate the Bar, and which Trinity House declined. In the end Trinity House advertised for tenders, and Bragg won the contract for a fortnightly service from Clovelly at £60 per annum, plus £2 per extra trip. From then on the supply arrangements for Trinity House and Heaven were separate, and Bragg continued to serve Trinity House with his skiff *Ranger* until the end of 1877, when he retired. He applied for a pension in view of his long service, but that was refused and Cox, with his *Chance* out of Appledore, was appointed in his place. He continued in the service until 1897, and the Heaven family described him as very civil and obliging. There are several references in the Heaven diary to crossings which took twenty-two hours or more, when the boat was forced to anchor overnight, or difficult landings made at Hell's Gates or Pilot's Quay.

---

**Trinity House Service Lundy Island**

Tenders are invited from Parties desirous of contracting to supply CRAFT HIRE to attend upon the Lighthouse and Fog Gun Stations at Lundy Island, by fortnightly trips during the year, namely, on the First and Fifteenth days of each month, Weather permitting. Tenders, stating particulars as to description and size of craft proposed to be used, number of crew, port sailing from, and annual sum required for the work, to be forwarded by post to the Secretary, Trinity House, London EC, on or before the 10th day of November, 1873.

Charges for extra trips to the island, and trips with ammunition to the Fog Gun Station, to be quoted separately in the Tender.

(Ilfracombe Chronicle 1873)

---

Lundy gradually became more accessible during the 1870s as the number of pleasure steamers bringing day-trippers to the island increased. Although the sometimes-rowdy visitors were not welcome to the Heaven family, the convenience of the extra facility for travel directly from the channel ports during the summer, without the necessity of making the long detour by land to Ilfracombe, Bideford or Clovelly, lessened their reluctance to permit landing. For the island inhabitants, the steamers meant that there were more opportunities to make visits to the mainland or to receive visits from friends and relatives, and it can be imagined that the augmentation of company was welcome to the small population. Such visits also served to keep the islanders in touch with news and happenings on the mainland. By the 1880s and 90s the paddle steamers from Bristol, South Wales or Portishead came regularly during the summer seasons. They called at Ilfracombe to disembark some of their passengers and to pick up others for the Lundy trip; later in the day the steamer returned to Ilfracombe before departing up-channel. The popular Lundy trip proved a useful way for the steamship owners to maximise their returns, as otherwise they would have been waiting all day at Ilfracombe. As the lighthouse was so prominent, many of those day-trippers would have wanted a guided tour by one of the keepers or a member of their families.

The landing bay with paddle steamer, before 1897 (Heaven archive)

Lundy lighthouse was one of the stations where it was thought desirable to replace the sperm oil used for the lamps by paraffin, which had been developed after the strike of oil in Pennsylvania in 1859. The new fuel was cheaper than sperm oil, and was also more volatile and less viscous, which made drawing up the oil to the wicks easier. But paraffin needed an increased supply of air to burn properly. A solution was found to this problem in 1868 which enabled paraffin to come into general use, and arrangements were made for the lighthouse barracks, no longer in use, to be converted for the storage of the mineral oil.

The new gunners who followed Lee and Blackmore in 1873, Morgan (the principal) and James, brought no children with them. They were described as "a knave and a fool". Nineteenth century religiosity is reflected in a long description of James (Crespi 1881), who was evidently a teetotaller:

> "...in two lonely cottages live two men...Day by day, all through the year, one of these men is on watch waiting for the fog; all through the night, fine or wet, cold or warm, every ten minutes one of these men walks from his cottage and looks out; if it is at all thick or dark he has to descend a long, steep flight of steps, from the bottom of which he can, if it be clear, see the lantern; if he cannot see the latter he knows it is thick, and he then fires off a rocket, and sometimes for several days and nights the rockets are going incessantly...One of these men — Thomas James — has for years worked like a hero at his post; never wavering, never failing...[he] is no puny lad, he is a huge, broad-shouldered, upright man of enormous strength...He stands 5 ft 9 in, or a little more, and weighs a good — a very good — 200 lb. How does he keep up his strength, how keep his spirits from failing, how bear the exposure? Well, mighty are the home-baked loaves, huge pots of tea, and large the dishes of vegetables which he and his sturdy wife consume...He is happy, though, — a wise, good man, contented to be poor...the wages of James are small; of course being in Trinity House employ he has many perquisites, house, coals, light and uniform, but many a Birmingham mechanic receives more money for a day's work then he for a week...but he pays his own way, owes no man a farthing..."

In 1874 the visiting captains reported that the lighthouse establishment was in a very neglected and unsatisfactory condition, with the sole exception of Maskell's dwelling.

However helpful to ships, the shining light was an unaccustomed hazard to the birds and AK Reece caught 100 blackbirds and thrushes on one occasion in February 1874. Later that year, a summary report of the committee's visit to Lundy provides some details that illustrate the range of their concerns, beginning with a disciplinary matter (THGLA 1874):

> "Light Committee to remove Chavener, Assistant keeper, to a Rock Station and James, Asst Gunner, to a Light Vessel and to be placed at the bottom of the List of Lamplighters, also to arrange with Mr Douglass for the supply of a New Lamp for the High Light House, a new fire place for the Principal Keeper's dwelling, the raising of the Back chimney staff of the Fog Gun Station Dwelling a few feet, the repair of the pipe thereat leading from the Tank to the W. Closet and the erection of Pig Sties for the use of the Gunners."

Gunner Morgan with rocket apparatus (Heaven archive)

The nature of the two men's offence is not specified, but the trouble must have been serious as the principal keeper and the other lighthouse assistant were also moved shortly afterwards. The Heaven family would have been particularly sorry for the departure of Thomas and Mary James, who had been frequent helpers with various island tasks. James was a shoemaker, "...kindly, good-natured, honest and religious", and his wife "...an obliging, useful good woman" who helped at the Villa from time to time, and who joined in the social sewing afternoons. Possibly they were later exonerated, as they returned to Lundy in 1876 and stayed until 1890. Mr Howgego, the PK, had also been useful to the family in many capacities, including decorating the Villa, while Mrs Howgego joined the sewing afternoons, and her two children, Harry and Harriet, were often companions to the two Heaven children and shared their lessons. Howgego was replaced by Roberts as PK, but it was noted in the Heaven diary that his family had refused to accompany him to Lundy. As recommended, the pigsties were built and the ruins lie just above the path down to the Battery.

Meanwhile, pilot skiff number 19 was lost in 1874, as well as the *Providence,* which sank off the north end after being abandoned by the crew, who were unable to pump out the large quantity of water in the hold. She was judged not to have been seaworthy. The SS *Fingal* went ashore at the south end of the island in thick weather; fortunately she had been running dead slow, and although she was damaged forward she was towed off and taken to Ilfracombe. In September the *Fanny,* which had come to collect cattle, was driven onshore by a north-easterly wind and was a total wreck; once again the islanders were busy wrecking on the beach.

The year 1875 is without any record of wrecks, but at the beginning of 1876 a French schooner *Jean et Robert* carrying coal from South Wales, lay at anchor close in the Roads. She was driven onshore by easterly winds with three lives lost, and by the next morning the ship was shattered to pieces. The farm bailiff rescued three men and one managed to get ashore where they were clothed, warmed and fed. More than two tons of coal was recovered with PK Robert's permission as deputy Receiver of Wreck. He was however angered by the thieving from the wreck, and that the wrecking continued for weeks.

The shipment of gunpowder from Clovelly was forbidden in 1876 for safety reasons, and so arrangements were made for it to be stored and supplied from Pembroke. This arrangement only lasted for two years as experiments with the use of gun-cotton rockets were successful. It was therefore decided to install them on Lundy to replace the guns. After some debate it was decided they should be installed at the fog gun station, and not the lighthouse. Four-ounce cotton powder rockets were to be used, as it was found that they gave a louder signal than the guns. The rockets also fired to a height of 600 feet, making them audible over a greater distance. As four ounces of powder was used instead of the three pounds of gunpowder needed for the guns, the rockets were also much more economical.

The method of use was that the projection and ringed piece of the quill were coated with an inflammable material similar to that on a present-day match, and the long tube, stopped at one end, was filled with powder. A piece of string was tied to the ring, and when the tube was inverted in the touch-hole of the barrel the string was pulled, the friction ignited the inflammable coating, fired the powder in the tube, and set off the gun. The question was raised as to whether the cannons should be removed, but the War office was informed that removal would be both difficult and expensive, with the result that they remain at the Battery today.

For purposes of safety, the Rocket is supplied, and is to be kept, in three parts, viz:-

1.  THE ROCKET This is a case charged with the ordinary rocket composition, and is intended merely to carry up the explosive charge to the required height, and then to ignite the detonator which is to explode the cotton powder.

2.  THE DETONATOR. This is an enlarged percussion cap, filled with fulminate. Its duty is to cause an explosion to take place in the heart of the cotton powder charge, whereby that charge is exploded. The detonator is ignited by the burning of the Rocket composition.

3.  THE COTTON POWDER CARTRIDGE. This is the explosive which produces the report, and which, with the detonator placed inside it, is to be fitted in the head of the Rocket, when immediately required for use.

The fitting together of the three parts can be accomplished in less than a minute; the rocket is then lighted by applying an ordinary fuse to a piece of Bickford fuse, communicating with the Rocket composition. The whole operation occupies less than two minutes. The cost of the Rocket is about 1s. 5d., whereas each discharge of the gun costs 2s.; and in foggy weather a Rocket is sent up every ten minutes. The advantages gained by the introduction of the sound Rocket are indisputable...

The explosive charge is carried up to the height of about 600 feet, and is there caused to explode in free air. From the height at which the explosion takes place, the sound is sent downwards into places which would be completely hidden from the level at which a Gun could be fired, and which would seldom be reached by the sound of its discharge...

It should also be mentioned that the charge of the Gun was 3 lbs of powder, and that the explosive charge of the Rocket consisted of four ounces of cotton powder.

(Findlay 1885)

The schooner *Ethel* was lost in fog when she struck Black Rock in February 1877. She sank within minutes, and of the crew of 20 only the mate survived. He was swept overboard, but managed to swim ashore in his cork jacket. He then scaled the cliff, and presented himself at the Heavens' Villa. His deposition was taken by the PK of the lighthouse, Edward Roberts, as deputy Receiver of Wreck. (The bell from this vessel now hangs in the island tavern.)

We reported yesterday that the steamer *Ethel* had sunk off Lundy island in a dense fog, and that all hands, excepting one, had been lost. She struck on the Lundy rocks at about 5.30 on Tuesday morning. There was a heavy sea running at the time. In a few moments the ship went down, with the greater number of the crew, while the rest were tossed about among the breakers. The only soul that survived was the mate, who, with a life-belt round him, clung to one of the ship's boats until that was broken to pieces among the rocks. At last, in the course of an hour, the tide cast him on to the shore thoroughly exhausted.

(The Times 1877)

One of the two cannons at the Fog Signal Station (courtesy of R. Derek Sach)

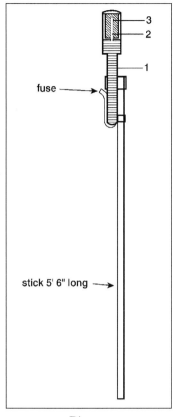

<table>
<tr><td>fuse</td><td>→</td></tr>
</table>

3
2
1
fuse →
stick 5' 6" long →

Diagram
of rocket apparatus

Trinity House efforts to secure a medical officer (or a replacement officer) for its personnel on Lundy were only partially successful. Dr Ackland of Bideford was said to have been a man of deep concern for all his patients, no matter their class, and had made house-to-house visits during an outbreak of cholera. He had been joined in his work by Charles Kingsley during the time he spent at Bideford in 1854–55, and the two went to Lundy in a fishing boat during a storm to visit an emergency case. By 1878 Ackland was not a young man, and was aware of the difficulties of attending patients on Lundy. He agreed to be appointed medical officer to attend Trinity House patients in Bideford for the regulation fees, but on condition that each visit made to the island would be paid separately. However, in 1884 he declined to visit a patient at the lighthouse as that was not part of his agreement with Trinity House, and so the securing of urgent medical treatment was again a problem. Between 1876 when William Hudson Heaven suffered a severe stroke and 1883 when he died, there was a doctor on the island, as a resident physician attended him. With light duties for Mr Heaven's doctor, it could be supposed that he was engaged by the islanders when necessary (although it would hardly have been possible for many of them to afford the fees).

One of the resident doctors caring for Mr Heaven was a Dr Crespi. He published an article in 1881 in *The Temperance Record* in which he compared the admirable Thomas James at the fog signal station, "a wise, good man...a remarkable instance of health and strength, of patient devotion to duty, of thrift, sobriety, and piety" to "Trinity House servants [who] are muddled half their time, too drunk to go on duty, head over ears in debt...far from respectable members of the community". This allegation caused a furore on the island. Trinity House began an enquiry but the fuss eventually blew over. It was, however, impossible for Crespi to continue to live on Lundy.

The matter was revived in January 1882, when AK Maskell was reported by PK Parsons for drunkenness and was dismissed from the service. He went with his wife to bid goodbye to Mr Heaven and his family, and was said to be "very sorrowful". He was replaced by Wilson, who arrived with his wife and baby. PK Parsons had previously replaced Roberts, and had arrived with his wife and six children in 1879, and Brown had been replaced by Whitchurch in 1880, who arrived to take up his duties with three children and his wife. She had another baby at Lundy in October of the following year, but unfortunately he died within a few days and was buried at the north end of the ancient graveyard which lies alongside the lighthouse. When the third keeper, Wilson, was taken ill and had to get to hospital there was an easterly wind, and he could not be taken off from the beach. He was taken in a hay cart to a point just north of the Fog Signal Station, and from there he was lowered on a hurdle into the boat. It is a steep and rocky stretch of coast, and the manoeuvre would have demanded skill and courage of every man involved. For the lighthouse families there must have been many times of great anxiety when they or their children were ill, although the Reverend Heaven was said to have been skilled in first aid and he kept a comprehensive medicine chest.

In 1880 it was decided that wind registers should be kept at Lundy, adding another burden to the lot of the light keepers. At about that time Lloyds began representations for temporary premises to be allowed on Trinity House land to enable them to set up an experimental reporting station, but that was refused. Three losses in 1880–81 were all vessels that sank as a result of collisions: the *Rattler*, the *Marco Polo,* and the *Cambronne,* or *Cambrian,* which was run down by the *Marian* behind Lamatry. She went down with all hands except for the captain and two others who were picked up by a tug, while the *Marian* gave no assistance. In October of the same year a burning vessel was seen near the island, for which there are no details.

The *Paola Ravello* ran ashore in fog in August 1882 below the quarries. She was pulled off by tugs, but found to be so damaged that she was towed to the beach and 70 tons of coal was discharged. On that occasion the members of the crew were at Lundy for sixteen days, and cordial relations were established with the Heaven family. Visits were made by and to the captain, and there was an exchange of island produce in return for Italian wine as well as trading in books. It was rumoured that this wreck had also been an insurance matter, though the captain denied it. The island was left with about 70 tons of coal from the wreck.

At the end of the year, two vessels were lost due to fog. The first was the *Burnswark* on the east side near Quarter Wall, where the crew had to abandon ship and were taken off by a pilot cutter from a total wreck. Plundering of spirits, porter and tobacco went on at night. Although the crew had said that the cargo was of rich silks and velvets "destined for an African king", the islanders were very disappointed when the wooden cases were found to contain only household glass. The *Heroine* struck on Seal Rock at the northeast of the island but the crew took to their boats, were able to climb the cliffs, and were housed on the island with the crew of the *Burnswark*. Nine of them went back to the ship at low water to retrieve their belongings, but when they failed to return it was thought they must have drowned. But a few days later the smiling captain reappeared; they had been carried westward of Lundy by a strong current, and picked up by a vessel going up-channel. The wrecking after the disaster of these two vessels had been of such proportions that a notice was put up in the store concerning unlawful theft.

---

**Wreck Sale**
**Appledore, North Devon**

To be sold by AUCTION, for the benefit of those concerned, the HULL of the Barque, "BURNSWARK," of 253 tons register, now lying stranded at Lundy Island, and all her Ropes, Sails, Stores, Patent Topsail Yards, Patent Bower Anchors and others, Standing and Running Rigging, Warps, Hawsers &c., and about 500 Boxes of Brass Rods and other salved portions of the Cargo, now landed at New Quay Yard, Appledore, for the Convenience of Sale.

The whole of the above will be offered for Sale by MR GEORGE BAKER, on the NEW QUAY, Appledore, North Devon on THURSDAY, the 18th inst., at 11 a.m. for 12 precisely, in suitable Lots.

(North Devon Journal 1883)

---

1883 began with the wreck of an unidentified barque and a steamer at the south end of the island. In September the *Little Ruth* landed on the beach due to fire, but she was safely refloated soon after. During the following year, the *Hornet* sank in a force nine gale after developing a leak. Both the SS *Wimbledon* and the SS *Baines Hawkins* struck the east side in thick fog and were stranded. On 27th July there was a single reference in the diary to an un-named steamer having struck the rocks and sunk.

In January 1884 (Heaven Archive 1884) there was a

"furious hurricane sort of storm ...the lighthouse struck by lightning...the dwelling-house suffered principally, no one hurt. 15 panes of glass broken...Whistles of communication spoiled...The lighthouse first struck they think at iron chimney of stove in tower. Lightning conductor crossed twice apparently by electric fluid in its vagaries but failed to conduct, granite of building scored as if by a chisel in the sand."

Report of enquiry into the loss of the American brigantine *Heroine*, 450 tons, on 13 December 1882, which left Newport with a crew of ten loaded with a cargo of 700 tons of coal:

In the evening the weather became hazy, and a fresh breeze set in from the east. At that time the master was of opinion that he was abreast of Lundy Island. But the night was too dark and the weather too thick to enable him to see the lights on Lundy. The weather thickened and the course of the vessel was altered to west. The chief officer then took charge of the ship, but he did not know the position of the vessel, except what the master told him. The west course was continued, and as they seemed to be impressed with the conviction that they were fast heading away to the Atlantic no lead was used. About half past 11 o'clock the vessel struck the ground on the east point of Lundy Island. All hands were soon on deck, but it was evident that she had struck something, and a hole was being made in her bottom. She was got off, but when the pumps were sounded 3 feet of water was found in her hold, and notwithstanding the efforts of the crew, the water gained rapidly upon them. The boat was got out, and when it seemed that there was no chance of saving the vessel, the crew took to the boat and landed on the island, and a few minutes afterwards the vessel went down…there were no lights on this side of the island, and the Board of Trade desired the court to say whether, in their opinion, a light ought to be placed there. The master was of opinion that had there been a light, he must have seen it, and that would at once have told him his position…The court were of opinion that the evidence before them was insufficient to enable them to come to a conclusion whether a light on the side of Lundy Island where the vessel was wrecked was necessary or not. They were of opinion that the master was to blame…He had hitherto borne an excellent character as the master of a vessel, and had been rewarded for saving life at sea. Under these circumstances, his certificate would only be suspended for three months.

[Newspaper cutting, un-named and not dated]

Repairs to the landing place were carried out, but at the expense of a project to improve the one on the west at Pilot's Quay.

Early in 1884 Mr Heaven granted Lloyds the lease of a signals site adjoining the castle, and the telegraph connection was set up. This was a great event for Lundy, which made a huge difference not only for ships' masters and owners, but also for all the islanders, since messages could be sent or received without having to wait for the chance of a boat, or having to rely on a beacon for summoning a doctor when urgently needed. Two rather out-of-place semi-detached cottages were built near the castle, and another family was added to the island population. As Lloyds' signalmen were on watch, albeit with views only eastward and south-ward, it seems probable that this was of some support to the light keepers, who were also able to cable information to the mainland very quickly.

Lloyd's Signal Station
in 1909, sited above
the landing bay
(Heaven archive)

The number of wrecks between the installation of the Fog Signal Station in 1862 and the end of 1884 was 64, and Trinity House was still exercised by the problem of fog, as well as the problem with the lighthouse. As the Fog Signal Station was sited low down on the western cliffs, the keepers there could not see if there was any fog on the plateau, or the north, south or east sides. Nor did the range and audibility of the rockets give effective warning to ships to the east, north or south of the island. There were varying proposals to connect the lighthouse and the signal station by telephone, or to install rockets at the lighthouse to alert the signal station to fog on the east side (the measure eventually adopted). But in December 1884 it was decided that sanctions should be sought for building two new lighthouses at a low level, one at each end of the island, and that £2,500 for each lighthouse should be included in the estimates for the next year. The new lighthouses would replace the existing light and signal station, would be equipped with first-class fog signals, and would be built at an estimated cost of £16,000 each.

### The Dangers of Lundy Island — Inaccuracy of the Admiralty Sailing Directions

At the Swansea Guildhall on Saturday afternoon a Board of Trade enquiry into the circumstances attending the stranding of the steamships *Wimbledon* and *Bains Hawkings* on Lundy Island on the 27th ult. was concluded. It appeared that the steamships left Cardiff on the 26th June with cargoes of coal, and when they arrived off the Bull Light a dense fog came on. The steamships proceeded straight on their course, taking the channel between Lundy and the Devonshire coast, and, since the soundings here are very equable, their commanders did not think it necessary to take a cast of the lead, especially as the sailing directions issued by the Admiralty informed them that a detonating rocket is fired off from Lundy every ten minutes during a fog and that it can be heard for fifteen miles. They did not hear the rocket, and therefore thought they were far from the island. Evidence was taken of Trinity House officials stationed on the island, and these swore that directly the fog was seen on the west side of the island detonating rockets were regularly fired. It is not possible for a fog to prevail on one side of the island and not the other, and for it to be seen on shore and not on the sea, and vice versa. The signalling station is on the west side, whereas the accident occurred on the east — the side generally used by navigators — and since there are no authorised means of obtaining information from this side, it is quite possible for an accident to occur on the east side without any of the Trinity House officials knowing it. All these witnesses expressed the opinion that so far as the east side is concerned the signalling is useless, and that if the sailing directions declared the rocket could be heard 15 miles on all sides, they were misleading. It is a curious coincidence that the two steamships ran aground on the same spot at almost the same time. The court found the master and first mate of the *Wimbledon* and the master of the *Bains Hawkings* in default, but considering the extraordinary circumstances connected with the case, decided not to deal with their certificates. It is the intention of the court to make a representation to the authorities with regard to the inadequate signalling arrangements on Lundy.

(Bideford Gazette 1884)

# Chapter 7

## The Old Light extinguished: 1884–97

John McCarthy arrived on Lundy in 1884 with his wife and six children. A seventh child, Augustus, was born not long afterwards. The family lived in the four-roomed PK's cottage, and McCarthy's great grandson wrote (Le Messurier 1992):

> "It was no real handicap for children to be on the island. There were several other boys and girls of school age…and the Squire who taught the boys had been a Taunton headmaster before taking up residence on Lundy. The girls were taught twice weekly by his sister, Miss Amelia Heaven, or by his cousin, Miss Annie Heaven…Church services were held in the Manor Farm at 4 pm on Sundays…Life on the island was carried on under the benevolent rule of Squire Heaven…the Rev. Hudson Grosett Heaven, B.A… Every day he walked across to the lighthouse with his dogs from the Villa…and stopped to chat with Mary McCarthy and the children. At Christmas he gave each child a present…The boys especially enjoyed life on the island. 'Egging' was the favourite pursuit, and meant being lowered over the cliff on the end of a rope. The younger children and the girls had to be content with robbing the puffins' nests in the old rabbit burrows. All the children had jobs to do for their mother. There [was] the wash-house copper to be stoked, water to be pumped from the wells, the chickens to be fed, and sewing to be done in the evenings."

A heavy job was to haul their coal, which was unloaded from a collier at the beach, and was an operation that took eight days to complete. It also took an entire day to carry the oil cans from the beach to the lighthouse, but those tasks were not carried out by the keepers.

The limitations of the fog signal system were highlighted with the loss of the tug *Peer of the Realm* in fog on the east side below Templar Rock, on 11th February 1885. An inquiry followed during which the firing and audibility of the fog signals were questioned, and Morgan was called ashore to give evidence. The efficacy of the fog signals was investigated, and by a trial exercise it was found that two out of three of the signals could not be heard. Following that there were suggestions that the rockets should be re-sited to the top and centre of the island, or that another fog signal station should be built on the east side. No more was recorded about that either, perhaps to avoid the extra expense when there were already plans in hand for the new lighthouses. Despite attempts to raise her, the *Peer of the Realm* had to be abandoned. The Heaven diary (Heaven Archive 1885) provides an interesting viewpoint on events:

> "The shipwrecked crew…got at the brandy and raved and fought and ill-tongued about hideously…14th…agent came…Fred [Ward] and G. Thomas warders of the vessel. Of course thieving has prevailed as usual. Dreadfully densest fog pressing white and woolly up to the windows."

In 1885 a small iron-clad church was built on the island, with a Sunday school nearby for the children. This original church was a small, pre-fabricated corrugated iron building. The Heaven diary shows that the Trinity House men and their families took part in island events and functions, and that they often acted as a supplementary work force. There was a party at the Villa each Christmas for the island children, where they all received presents. On one occasion the young Augustus McCarthy from the lighthouse was presented with a velvet suit and was made to put it on at once, much to his embarrassment. The Heaven family, particularly the Reverend Heaven, called upon the lighthouse regularly and, much less formally, all the other islanders socialised in the stores and Refreshment Room (where the Heaven children were forbidden to go, as alcohol was served there). Among exchange visits and social occasions, events involving all the islanders included, for example, bank-holiday festivities. For the celebration of the Queen's Jubilee in 1887 there was a church service followed by the national anthem, then tea for everyone at the farmhouse, after which there were sports with prizes and, lastly, a bonfire and dancing.

The church at the top of Millcombe, 1885, which could hold more than 60 people. It was dedicated (not consecrated) as it stood on private land, and therefore marriages and confirmations could not be celebrated there (Heaven archive)

When shooting parties were organised for the Heaven family, the Trinity House men were given the option of going out as beaters, in return for which they were lent guns during the rest periods to shoot rabbits and were allowed to keep their bag. Similarly, the lighthouse and fog signal men and their families are recorded as helping with haymaking, decorating, shoe mending, laundry work and other tasks (although one or two attempts to give the elder children employment as servants met with a marked lack of success). In return, the islanders got medical first-aid, the loan of books, the observation of religious services, and counsel when needed. It seems that the lighthouse personnel, being better educated than the island labourers and not island employees, fulfilled a useful intermediate role between the squire and his family and the others.

The story of the lighthouse is sketchy from 1885–97 as Trinity House minutes were yet again curtailed in length and give only reference numbers as opposed to details of the subjects under consideration. The pressure on expenditure in 1886 forced the removal from the budget of the £5000 that was to have been set aside for the new Lundy lighthouses. In 1885 Mr Thomas Wright had taken the lease of the farm and store, and he complained to Trinity House in 1887 that rockets had caused a fire on his property and requested compensation for the damage. Trinity House refused to accept any responsibility, but Wright demanded a meeting, which turned out to be unsuccessful in resolving the matter. The dispute was passed to solicitors, and it took two years before a settlement of £25 was agreed, although by then the costs most probably exceeded the award originally sought. He also complained to the Board that the light keepers were trading. In what commodities they were trading was not recorded, but the keepers denied it and the matter was smoothed over.

The farmhouse around 1885 with the tenant, Mr Wright, on the left. The central portion (the Old House) was built in 1775–76 and the far left wing was added in 1863–68 by the Lundy Granite Company (Heaven archive)

With the support of Trinity House and Lloyds, Mr Wright made application to the GPO for the establishment of a postal service to Lundy with a sub-post office on the island. Although it was hardly likely to produce a profit, it was agreed that this should be done as a particular service to the island. The initial service from Cardiff proved to be chaotic, but once transferred to the island boatman at Instow there was a regular weekly service (weather permitting) which continued until 1927. The advantage to the Trinity House personnel was considerable in that not only could they receive direct letters and parcels, but the sub-post office sold stamps and postal orders and, later, postcards.

Apart from the expense of necessary improvements, Trinity House faced constant expenditure for maintenance. Not only for the road, which was trouble enough, but also for the lighthouse and signal station, which were both positioned on the west of the island facing the prevailing westerly gales. At the end of 1887 there was a particularly strong gale, and repairs were necessary to the lighthouse. The flagstaff, which stood at the southwest corner of the compound, had to be replaced. At that time the question of constructing a harbour of refuge in the Bristol Channel, possibly at Lundy, was raised once again, and another burden was proposed for the keepers' lives when they were instructed to keep a record of all vessels taking shelter. In bad weather, the number of vessels in the bay had been anything up to a hundred or so. However, this came to nothing; the Commissioners on Harbours of Refuge in 1858 had found that (Allington *et al.* 1994):

> "The trade of the Bristol Channel comprises nearly one-sixth of the shipping...of the entire United Kingdom, ...[but] at Lundy Island is to be found a site in every respect well adapted for such a harbour, except the important one of expense — the depth of water...is so great as to occasion a cost of construction not to be thought of..."

After the *Peer of the Realm* wreck in 1885 there were eleven wrecks during the period 1886–1889, including two in fog that were not identified. There is a mystery over the schooner, *Bosweden,* which was seen off Lundy on 15th October 1886 but nothing further was ever heard of her. Then the full-rigged *Inversnaid* was seen by two tugs listing to the west of Lundy in a force 10 northerly gale, but the master did not consider her to be in danger. The sad result was that lifebuoys and two small boats from the vessel were later washed ashore at Peppercombe. In the same gale the *Juanita* was lost without a trace, except for wreckage washed up at Bideford. In 1888 three more vessels were wrecked in fog. The *Electric* struck at Pilot's Quay on the west side and broke up after the crew had managed to get off. Another un-named ship also struck nearby, but was able to get off without serious damage, and the *Elsie* struck on the east side. The pilot cutter *New Prosperous* ran onshore to the north of the landing place, a total loss. The *Radnor* was also wrecked in 1888. There was one wreck in 1889, the schooner *Eliza Jones* lost with her crew of three.

Gunner James made a daring descent of the cliffs from the Battery in September of 1890 to assist two boats round to the landing beach with survivors of the wreck of the *Ashdale*, which had foundered just off Lundy. Subsequently there was a Board of Trade enquiry into the loss of this ship, and PK McCarthy wrote to give evidence that there had been an accident in the engine room which filled with water, and that one of the ship's boats was very old. The verdict of the enquiry was that the master had been at fault by not operating the pumps before abandoning ship, and his certificate was suspended for six months. His appeal was dismissed, but he was not forced to pay costs. It was suspected that the ship had been sunk intentionally, but that was not proven. The tenant, Mr Wright, was furious over a newspaper article that reported he had failed to provide any food for the survivors, who had been properly looked after on the island. Yet another grounding in fog followed, the SS *Ackworth,* whose crew was brought to land safely before the ship sank the next day.

At the Fog Signal Station cottages, 1887. L to R: Chief Gunner Morgan,
Mrs Morgan, their adopted daughter Annie who was visiting for the
christening of her baby, and Gunner James (Heaven archive)

Later in 1890 James and his wife left Lundy ("poor Mrs James very tearful") to be replaced by Mr Banner and his wife. Mrs Morgan was taken ill in March 1892 and when her condition gave rise to alarm, the doctor was sent for. He arrived the next day, but was too late to give her any assistance. She died of bronchitis, and according to the doctor, was "wholly worn out". In June, Morgan bade Mr Heaven and his family goodbye after nineteen years on Lundy, and Mr Paul arrived at the battery in Morgan's place.

A decision was made in November of 1892 that funds should be conserved for the new lighthouses rather than expended on improvements. In the meantime, however, Trinity House was in the vexatious situation of balancing this edict with their responsibility for the efficiency of warning systems and avoidance of wrecks. Decisions had been complicated by another cancellation of the set-aside funds from the 1888–89 budget. But in the 33 years between 1859 and 1892, there had been 161 wrecks on Lundy.

The wreck of the *Elsie* early in 1888 was the subject of another enquiry, as it was claimed that no fog signals had been heard, and Trinity House submitted copies of the weather reports for the date of the stranding. As the Board of Trade did not approve the proposal for work to be started on the new lighthouses during 1889, Trinity House took measures to increase the power of the light, and to accelerate the revolution to a flash every minute instead of every two minutes, at a cost of £185. Another proposal to set up an additional explosive fog signal either at the lighthouse or at the northeast point was not approved.

Problems were exacerbated in 1892 when there were further complaints about the fog signals: the master of the *Bygda* asserted that no signal had been heard the previous December, and when the *Ackworth* ran ashore in fog in April, the same complaint was made. The wreck of the *Tunisie* in March of the same year took place in a gale and blinding snowstorm, with freezing temperatures, and the islanders carried out a truly heroic rescue of the twenty-two crew.

Among the rescue team was PK McCarthy. A rescue apparatus was rigged up using a signal rocket to carry a rope, with a coal sack adapted to make a breeches-buoy. The wreck occurred at 6 am, and the men did not return until the evening, exhausted and frozen. They were rewarded with a grant of 15*s* per man made by the National Lifeboat Institution, and McCarthy received a framed citation. The Elder Brethren conducted the presentation ceremony at the lighthouse at the curious hour of 6 am, and the Heaven diary laconically recorded that "not all the men went up". There appears to have been some disagreement over whether McCarthy or an islander, George Thomas, had been leader of the rescue. In July the Board of Trade's recognition consisted of £3 for every man, except George Thomas, the fisherman and general factotum, who is referred to as having organised the rescue. He received a silver medal but no money, and was heard to remark that the medal was handsome enough, but the money would have been of much more use to a working man with a family.

A more important upshot of the *Tunisie* wreck was that it drew attention to the fact that there was no rescue apparatus on the island. Consequently the island men were recruited to form a life-saving crew. By July of the following year the rescue apparatus arrived, a Commander Freeland came from the mainland to conduct the first rocket practice, and a hut to house the apparatus was built.

The telegraph cable had broken several times and was abandoned in 1888. So a very welcome improvement in communications was made in 1893 when the GPO installed a telephone cable. The lighthouse was connected to the telephone, which was installed in the cable hut built for that purpose against the north wall of the castle. Access to the island and haulage had been improved in 1892 when it was decided to extend the slipway, as it was in need of repair, and until then had consisted only of a narrow curved slope ending in steps to the beach. The cost of the works was £220 and was divided between Trinity House and the Reverend Hudson Heaven since it was of great advantage to both parties.

Rocket life-saving apparatus practice, around 1890 (Heaven archive)

There were recurrent problems with the water supply at the lighthouse, where tanks had been mounted to catch rainwater and feed it into three wells. The water tanks were cleaned out in 1883 and the water declared "very good". However, it was found necessary to open the drain from the PK's house and the pipes into the water tanks seven years later, as there had been complaints about the water and there was a bad smell in the AK dwellings. This fault, and Trinity House neglect in remedying it, had tragic consequences. In August of 1892 the visiting officers noted that nothing had been done about the water since the visit three years before. Since early 1891 there had been recurrent epidemics of illness affecting first the keepers and their families in particular, and then the islanders in general. At one point the keepers declared that their water was evil, and they were driven to fetching their water from the stream at the bottom of St John's Valley ("Lodore"). In April 1892, several of the islanders and virtually everyone at the lighthouse was ill, and the superintendent had to be called in to take over the light duties for twelve days. On 1st September Mrs Hast, wife of the assistant keeper, died suddenly. It took until June 1893 before the drains were cleared, and October before the estimate for two new 400-gallon water tanks was approved. Later it was found that the drains had been contaminating the water supply.

### The McCarthy Family's Departure from Lundy, 1893

The Trinity House steamer, the *Ready*, brought the relief keeper. By the time his luggage was landed, and the outgoing gear shipped, a stiff north-east wind was blowing and heavy seas were breaking on the landing beach.

The ship's boat was in danger of being smashed on the rocks, so a farm wagon was backed down the beach into the sea, much to the disgust of the horses, and from this improvised jetty the family slithered into the tossing boat.

In a welter of spray and spindrift, the McCarthy family left the island, which had been their home for nine years…None of them ever returned, but they always spoke of Lundy with great affection, and kept in touch with the Heaven family for many years.

(Messurier 1964)

The inhabitants of the Old Light and visitors around 1892. L to R: AK Hast,
R McCarthy, visitor, PK McCarthy, Lilly Hast, Miss Hall, AK Hall, Mrs Hall,
Mrs McCarthy, Janie McCarthy; Lilly McCarthy, Gussie McCarthy,
Louise McCarthy; Hall's son and visitor.

At that time the keepers' gardens, which were divided between the light
keepers and the gunners, were described as being very neat. Visitors who came
to see the island on the steamer *Velindra* were delighted to have been received
by the keepers with great courtesy, who showed them all around and explained
the working of the light apparatus.

In November 1892 a new tug was lost without trace, and one body was
recovered just off the island. There were three wrecks in 1893, including SS
*Charles W Anderson* which ran ashore on the beach. The *Ismyr* was anchored in
the Bay but blown onto the rocks of Rat Island in a force 9 north-easterly gale,
with the loss of two lives. The *Favourite* was seen to be in distress off Lundy but
then disappeared from view. Later, four of the crew who had taken to their
boat were picked up and taken to Swansea.

The collier *Marie* was lost in fog in 1895 just north of the landing place.
The Heaven diary commented that the crew had heard the rockets but thought
they were thunder; it was suspected that schnapps had been responsible. The
crew sent up a signal and started to jettison their cargo of coal. A boat put
off from the island to search for her and brought all the crew of 25 ashore.
The *Coila* sank after colliding with the SS *Catherine*. Another un-named ship

was lost while under tow at the end of the year. During the following May the *Kate*, which was carrying stone for the construction of a new church on Lundy, ran aground but was not badly damaged. She was pulled off and was back in service in July. In October, the Danish brigantine *Sastie* collided with the schooner *Emily* just off Lundy, and sank after one hour. The crew was taken aboard the *Emily* and landed at Newport.

The final decision to proceed with the new north and south lighthouses was taken in 1894, and the records from then until 1897 are mostly concerned with the sites, plans, sanctions from the Board of Trade, the appointment of personnel, arrangements for housing the workmen, and the arrival of keepers for the North Light. Little mention was made of the existing lighthouse or the Battery until the time came for them to be closed down at the end of 1897. Meanwhile the rate of loss at sea between 1893 and 1897 increased slightly to just over two per year.

In the last year of the Old Light the count of wrecks amounted to an extraordinary twelve. The loss of the *Dyfed* was followed by the dramatic rescue of the crew of three of the pilot cutter *Mystery*, which had been found in distress off Lundy and towed by a tug. The hawser broke and the cutter drifted away. However, despite the high sea that was running, the tug managed to get alongside and rescue the crew before their vessel sank.

One of the two new lighthouses which were brought into use last night is erected at the extreme north-west point of the island…It is 56 ft in height from base to vane, and the light, which is shown at an elevation of 165 ft above high water spring tides and is visible in clear weather at a distance of 19 miles, gives two white flashes, each only two-thirds of a second in duration, in quick succession, every 20 seconds. The intensity of this light is equal to 81,000 candles in clear weather, and this can be increased to an intensity of 121,500 candles in thick weather.

The fog signal is a powerful siren worked by oil engines, and it will give four blasts in quick succession of low and high notes alternately every two minutes. The other new lighthouse stands on the south-east point of the island…It is 52 ft in height, and will show a white revolving light every minute at an elevation of 175 ft above high water spring tides. It will be of an intensity of 40,000 candles in clear weather, increased to 60,000 candles in thick weather, and it will be visible under favourable conditions at a distance of 20 miles. The fog signal is an explosive, consisting of 4oz. of cotton powder, which will give a report every ten minutes. It will thus be seen that the limits of the island will now be clearly defined in clear and thick weather; that the lights and fog signals will be of equal assistance to both outward and homeward bound vessels, and that vessels seeking refuge will be more safely enabled to reach it.

(The Times 1897)

Principal Keeper McCarthy
and son Gussie, 1893
(Heaven archive)

The Old Light, with the three keepers in front of the tower. The PK's cottage
on the right was demolished in 1897 (Heaven archive)

In March there were three losses. The crew of the smack *Telephone* endured a dangerous rescue. The ship lost her anchors in Lundy Roads during a tremendous gale, was blown westwards, and eventually sighted from Hartland Point. The life-saving team started for the Point with the rocket apparatus, but was prevented from making headway by the trees that had fallen across the road during the gale. The telephone line at Hartland was down, so a cyclist took the message to alert the men at Clovelly. The crew was finally taken off by the lifeboat and landed at Clovelly. The lifeboat responded to another distress signal when the *Grimsby* sprang a leak off Lundy and took off the crew. The smack *Diamond* was run down by a steamer in the Roadstead at Lundy, which managed to pick up all the crew before she sank.

A very large steamer, the *Cam*, was another victim of dense fog when she ran ashore under Tibbets Point, on the east side. The impact was much less than might otherwise have been the case as some Trinity House workmen who were rowing to the north end shouted a warning, and the engines were reversed. When the tide rose she was floated off and taken to Barry. Three days later, the *Salado* ran ashore at the Knoll Pins on the east side in thick and foggy weather. Fortunately there was a tug in the bay which came to her assistance, and the crew of 22 and three passengers were landed on the island and taken to Ilfracombe the following day.

Less than two weeks later the ketch *Millicent* ran ashore and was lost, though her crew survived. There was a severe gale in May when the ketch *Infanta* was driven ashore and wrecked, but her companion vessel *Yeo* which had also struck, managed to throw a rope to a steamer which towed her off. The *Rover* was employed in salvage work on the *Salado* and was alongside when she was caught by a north-easterly gale and sank, heavily loaded. The last wreck during the final year of the Old Light was the SS *Ballydoon*. The *Ballydoon*, or *Bally Doone*, struck a submerged wreck, sprang a leak, and sank on the west side in an easterly gale.

The population of Lundy was greatly expanded and the island vibrant with activity in the years 1896 and 1897 when the two new lighthouses were being built. At the same time, a new granite-built church was under construction near the farmhouse. Trinity House built barracks to house their workmen at the north and south sites, with berths in tiers of three to house twenty-four men. There was a central living-room and a kitchen, and cooks were installed to cater for them, but there can be little doubt that the workmen would have augmented the company in the island refreshment room in their spare time.

Lundy South

Lundy North

17th November 1897 was the occasion of some sadness: the Heaven ladies

"went on the common near the church to take a last look at the old Lighthouse
Light — this is the last night of its shining - alas!"

The next evening Ann Mary Heaven drove in the carriage to the north
end with her cousin, the Reverend Hudson Heaven, and lit the lamp of the new
lighthouse. The Battery was closed down, the furnishings moved to the North
Light, and Mr and Mrs Banner left the island. The south lighthouse was still
equipped with a temporary light pending the transfer and installation of the
light apparatus from Beacon Hill, but by 10th December all was in place, and
the Reverend Heaven lit the lamp in the new lighthouse. The keepers from the
old lighthouse all chose to move to the new south lighthouse, rather than take
a new posting. The new lighthouses, manned by crews of four, were classed as
rock stations and the families had to leave. Duties were rotated with shore
leave, so that three keepers were in charge of each lighthouse at any one time.

With the exception of the eastern outbuilding, the principal's cottage and
the outbuildings had all been dismantled so that the stone could be used to build
the new South Light. After 77 years the Beacon Hill lighthouse remained only
as a daymark, and the keepers' quarters stood empty. The keys of the lighthouse
and the Fog Signal Station were handed to the owner of the island.

# Chapter 8

## Old Light — New History: *from 1897*

The lighthouse on Beacon Hill very soon became referred to as the Old Light. Trinity House had tried to exploit the return of the corporation's buildings in order to get favourable terms for a lease on the north and south sites. Negotiations dragged on and it was another two years before the deed was signed whereby all the old Trinity House sites were exchanged for the new ones. It may have been symbolic that the flagstaff at the Old Light was blown down and utterly broken.

In the 83 years between the installation of the north and south lighthouses at the end of 1897 and 1980 there were 21 wrecks, of which one was due to enemy action during the 1939–45 war, and only five are recorded as due to fog. One of these was the famous naval vessel HMS *Montagu*, the flagship of the home fleet. In the early hours of 30th May 1906 the keepers of the North Light were astonished when two somewhat dishevelled naval officers presented themselves at the door of the lighthouse. The ship had struck at the southwest corner of the island, and the two officers had rowed under the lea of the island towards the north, from where the fog signal could be heard. They had to find a place to land where they could climb the cliffs, and were more than astonished when the keepers told them they were at Lundy North. They were convinced that they had struck at Hartland and were somewhat reluctant to concede the point. While the marked drop in the number of wrecks undoubtedly reflects the much greater efficiency of the two new lighthouses with their foghorns, the introduction of wireless and radar have also played a part in reducing the number of marine accidents.

Because the Battery cottages have such steep access they have not been used since 1897, but the Old Light was not deserted. Mr Philip Napier Miles JP, a landowner of Kings Weston, took the lease in 1898 to use for family holidays. He was said to be sociable, pleasant and courteous, most popular with all who knew him, and a cultured, well-read man, with musical tastes. He paid £25 in the first year for the rental of the lighthouse, the outbuildings, and the cottage, and he installed two islanders, Mr and Mrs Williams, as caretakers to the cottage, with a wage of 17s a week. He moved in his furniture, including a piano, and the outhouse (now Old Light West) was rebuilt with three rooms to accommodate his servants. Usually the family spent a month on Lundy in the summer, although the visit of 1900 was curtailed when Mr Miles' attendant, Frank Taylor, fell over a cliff while egging and was killed.

HMS *Montagu* was wrecked in fog in May 1906 at the southwest of the island (Heaven archive)

The Miles family enjoyed social gatherings with the Heaven family, which by that time had diminished to the elderly Reverend Hudson Heaven, his sister Millie, and cousin Anne Mary. But when the island was put up for sale in 1906 Mr Miles gave notice to end his lease because the Williams wished to resign, and he felt that Lundy would simply not be the same without the resident family or with strangers at the Villa. The lease was terminated in September 1907. A draft agreement was drawn up for the then lessee, Taylor, to take over the Old Light, the cottages and land, at £34 a year, but it is uncertain whether this was completed. If it was, Taylor evidently did not enter into possession of the buildings, but as he hoped to take over the quarries he may have intended it for workers' accommodation. The granite option had already been taken up by another, however.

Lundy was put up for sale in 1906, and the writer of the catalogue of sale was moved to eloquence by the Old Light (Heaven Archive 1906), which

"...is naturally the most prominent object on the Island, and not only commands a view of the whole Island, but also a great expanse of sea, tracing the coastline of the mainland for many miles. The Lantern of the Tower provides a capital SMOKING ROOM and outlook. One cottage contains, on first floor, sitting room, three bedrooms and cupboard. Ground floor, sitting room, two bedrooms, two pantries. On the first floor of the Tower is a KITCHEN, and the lower Lantern is converted into a SCULLERY, and has a PUMP connected with rain-water reservoir. Outside is a stone and match-boarded BUNGALOW of three bedrooms, LARDER, COAL HOUSE, and near to another SMALL COTTAGE occupied by the Gardener and Caretaker of the Old Lighthouse. There is attached a large walled KITCHEN GARDEN."

What use may have been made of the Old Light between 1907 and 1917 is not known, except that the Heaven family for a time cultivated the gardens. When the island was sold to Mr A L Christie at the end of 1917, the Old Light was uninhabited. At that time Lundy was in a badly run-down state, with all the buildings and installations in need of repair, a radically reduced workforce, and the farm badly neglected. The Heaven family had long experienced a chronic shortage of both income and capital, and in their old age had been less able to manage matters. The Reverend Heaven and his cousin retired to the mainland in 1911, and his nephew, Walter Heaven, took over. He was however in debt and penniless, so did not have the ability to retrieve the situation. When he became owner in 1916, on the death of his uncle, the creditors foreclosed and the island had to be sold.

The purchaser, Augustus Langham Christie, of Tapeley, Instow, expended considerable capital in repairing the buildings, improving the water supply, re-establishing the farm, and improving the landing places. By 1920 Lundy was once more a working proposition, and it was leased to Mr Herbert May for five years. The Old Light was then sub-let as a private residence, where — at some time — the Plunkett Greene family took their holidays. Mr May was not resident, but he supervised the farm himself and appointed an efficient manageress, Miss Sage, for the farmhouse and hotel. Miss Sage was active in organising the social life of the islanders, together with four coastguards who had first been installed by the Admiralty in 1909. They had taken over signalling from Lloyds, and lived in cottages near the castle with their families.

The Harman family were the owners of Lundy from 1925–69. As a young man, Martin Harman visited Lundy and declared that he would, one day, buy it. He had progressed from office-boy at Lazard bankers to become a director, and from there set up his own business. He was very successful, and when Lundy came up for sale in 1925 he was able to realise his dream. Although he spent his working life in the City he was a true countryman at heart, who cherished Lundy as a haven for wildlife and a place of peace for his family. He regarded Lundy as independent of mainland authorities, but a loyal member of the British Empire, and was adamant in retaining what he regarded as its ancient rights. Consequently he dismissed the GPO and the Admiralty Coastguards, and issued his own "puffin" stamps and coins. The stamps are still in use to cover the cost of mail transport to the mainland, but the coins were ruled as illegal, and were withdrawn from use, although they still appear as collectors' items. More importantly, the legal case ended in the ruling that Lundy was indeed part of the United Kingdom (Gade, 1978).

During the time that the Harman family was in ownership, the lighthouse building was put to various uses. At first it was available to rent for holidays and was popular with larger groups, with those who preferred to self-cater or with those on a limited budget. Lundy was a very sociable place during that period. Mr Harman established the Tavern as the hub of island life, and there were many regular visitors to the hotel. It was the heyday of pleasure steamers that brought visitors and day-trippers from South Wales, the Bristol Channel and North Devon ports of call. The resident agent, F W Gade, described in his memoir (Gade 1978) convivial visits by the crews of trawlers and small ships. There was a twice-daily radio connection to the Coastguards at Hartland, and one of the rooms in the Old Light Tower housed the apparatus and became the radio room. Another innovation was the construction of a golf course in 1927, for which an equipment shed was built against the west wall of what is now Old Light West.

F. W. Gade at the radio telephone in the Old Light in the 1930s
(photograph by the late Harry Savory, Harman collection)

All that came to an end with the outbreak of war in September 1939. The Admiralty had already issued a requisition notice to take over the Old Light and by October Lieutenant Catchpole and six naval ratings were installed there. In March 1941, they were summoned to take in charge the crew of a German Heinkel which had crash-landed on the island just south of Halfway Wall. The five prisoners were taken back to the lighthouse, and later that day were put aboard the island boat *Lerina* and taken to Appledore. The men of the Admiralty contingent were, thus, some of the few who encountered the enemy on British soil.

Light keeper Guppy with the Heinkel III aircraft that crash-landed in 1941.
The crew survived and were taken to the mainland

Shortly after that another German plane crashed into the steep slope on the west side, and the naval party arrived on the scene to find the plane burning fiercely. Two of the crew had been trapped in the cockpit, two had crawled clear, and a fifth man was lying nearby, severely injured. A makeshift stretcher was used to bring him to the top, where he was put onto the island cart, and the three survivors were taken to the Old Light, where the injured man was given morphine. The next day they were taken to Appledore, where they met with a hostile reception from the local populace, but the injured man was well treated and survived the war. Sadly that year the naval party also had to attend a British Whitley bomber which crashed into the west side during fog with no survivors, and only one body could be recovered.

As the Old Light had been occupied by the Admiralty men, and running repairs had been carried out, it ended the war in better condition than the other island buildings, which had suffered from the lack of men and materials to repair weather damage. In 1946 Mr Harman, a keen naturalist whose ambition was to see Lundy as a nature reserve, co-founded the Lundy Field Society with Professor Harvey of Exeter University. Mr Harman, the Society's first president, was generous in endowing them with a start-up fund of £50 and giving the use of the Old Light free of charge for a headquarters and hostel. The invitation to membership (Lundy Field Society Archive 1946) stated that

> "The Lundy Field Society has been formed for the purpose of furthering the study and conservation of the fauna and flora of Lundy, and in particular of establishing a bird observation station....The establishment of a station on Lundy will also provide a base for a continuous biological survey of the fauna and flora of a most interesting island..."

Under the leadership of the first warden, Rowland Barker, the founder members were industrious both in raising funds, in assisting with the work of redecoration, and finding and installing equipment before the lighthouse was ready to open for the 1947 season. By present standards the comfort level was not high, with canvas beds, oil lamps, water pumps, primus stoves, and Elsan portable toilets, but a blaze was kept going in the stove in the communal living-room and good cheer prevailed.

Although the heligoland bird-trap that was built in Stoneycroft paddock was not immediately successful, the first annual report shows that the Society had made a good start in fieldwork and recording observations. Subsequent wardens and a growing membership continued to expand the Society's activities, and field studies broadened to include archaeology, historical, and marine studies. A workroom in the west outhouse, a ringing-room in the east outhouse and a small library were gradually accumulated. In 1951 the level of comfort was improved with the installation of bedsteads and calor gas lighting and heating, and the charge for one week's bed and board was raised from three to four guineas (£4 4s). After the sudden death of Mr Harman in December of 1954 a memorial fund was raised, which was used to refurbish and equip the west outhouse as a laboratory in his memory.

By 1968, financial problems for the Field Society became acute, and it was reluctantly decided that the Society could no longer afford to support either a resident warden or the upkeep of the Old Light buildings. The Society has continued its work on the island, and after the Old Light reverted to the owner it was maintained as hostel accommodation available for visiting groups. Following the untimely death of Mr Harman's son Albion, who had taken over management of the island, the family was forced to sell Lundy.

In 1969 it was acquired by the National Trust with a donation by Mr Jack Hayward, along with the vital undertaking by the Landmark Trust to lease the island, manage it, and restore the buildings. The lighthouse then continued as a hostel, which proved of particular advantage to groups of climbers, divers, and students. In 1980 the Landmark Trust began the complete restoration of the lighthouse and the keepers' quarters. The specialised metal work was entrusted to the Alco Engineering Company, and Mr Wallace Cooke described his first impressions (personal communication):

> "A rather sorry sight met our eyes. The magnificently built granite building…had obviously been neglected for many years, allowing water…to pour through the fractured copper roof and into the Tower."

The weather vane had to be removed and sent back to the factory for restoration, the roof was repaired, a new door was required to the outside balcony, and the rusted handrails were replaced. Inside the tower much of the half-inch thick glass and its housing, the ironwork, and many of the vertical tie rods which held the top structure to the top course of the granite tower all had to be replaced. The copper ventilating covers around the building had to be remade by the coppersmith, and about one hundred feet of the internal handrail to the cantilevered granite stairs were replaced. On the keepers' houses much of the lead work was renewed. Once the overall refurbishment had been carried out, the lighthouse stood proud and resplendent on the Lundy horizon once more.

The lantern room under repair, 1980 (courtesy of John Hinshelwood)

With the stewardship of the Landmark Trust, the Old Light entered a new phase. The quarters have been restored to two separate apartments preserving the original character and layout of the keepers' quarters. They provide electricity, kitchens and shower-rooms, and are available for letting to holidaymakers. The former laboratory has been refurbished for the accommodation of staff (Old Light West), and the small block opposite is a comfortable single-person cottage for holiday lettings (Old Light East). Visitors may climb the spiral steps up to the lantern room and from the surrounding ledge they can view the entire island as well as the coasts of Devon, Cornwall and South Wales — on a fine day. There has not been consensus over the number of steps to the lantern: Gosse stated that there were 126, Chanter gave 147, others 119, or Findlay and the author, 134.

The agent's cottage, at first called "the cottage in the garden", was used for staff after 1897. It has inexplicably been omitted from every census return up to 1901, neither does it appear to have had a name before it became Stoneycroft during the Harman ownership. It was one of the buildings repaired at the request of Mr May around 1920, and during the Harman ownership an extension was built at the back. In 1939 the naturalist, Richard Perry, stayed there with his wife for five months to observe the bird life, and wrote (1940) that

> "With its crumbling discoloured walls and bare floors, its leaking roof, smoking chimneys, and icy draughts, the cottage was less habitable than any shepherd's croft in the Western Isles."

It too has been carefully restored and refurbished by the Landmark Trust and now offers a holiday home for four. There is a granite-lined and covered well in the front garden, and to the east a walled garden which still shows a few remnants of the careful cultivation by the farmer John Ogilvie and his wife, who lived there until 1989 with their two daughters.

The enclosed area to the east of the lighthouse, now referred to as The Paddock, would have been cultivated by the keepers as part of their domestic economy to obviate the reliance on supplies of uncertain frequency from the mainland. It also provided an area where additional buildings could be built if needed. The 1886 Ordnance Survey map shows the area divided into nine plots, which were shared between the light keepers and the gunners. It also shows a number of small buildings around the internal perimeter which may have been tool sheds; only the ruins of twin huts on the south wall now remain. The dividing walls of the Paddock have been removed, and the area now provides rough grazing for sheep.

Perry (1946) described standing on the lantern gallery, an experience which remains unchanged:

"...the lantern of the Old Light was 570 feet above the breakers booming against the steep cliffs and sidings below...we could see more than forty miles south-west on a clear day to Trevose Head on the Cornish coast, and as far north-west to the sugarloaf stack of Skokholm off Pembroke. North was the Gower Peninsula, and east and south the high tors of Exmoor and Dartmoor and Bodmin. From our ninety-foot watch-tower we could look over the three-mile length of the Island, sunlit in a sparkling sea: a table-mountain half a mile across, sheering up four hundred feet from the sea on granite cliffs and stacks and shelving green sidings…On a clear, peaceful night, 'shamed into pettiness by the innumerable silences of stars'."

# Appendix 1

## LUNDY LIGHTHOUSE KEEPERS

| Year | PK | AK1 | AK2 | Notes |
|------|-----|-----|-----|-------|
| 1820 | James Cornish | William Rawle | | £80 per annum = £70 + £10 gratuity |
| 1839 | | John Phelps | | Rawle superannuated @ £31.10s per annum |
| 1840 | John Phelps | Samuel Boulden | | Cornish superannuated @ £31 10s per annum |
| 1843 | | George Monk | | Boulden dismissed; accused of stopping the light |
| 1845 | | | | Monk requested transfer, again in 1848, 1851, 1854 |
| 1847 | William Welch | | | Phelps moved to another station |
| 1849 | | | | Henry Reece (perhaps on temporary service) requested transfer as too tall for lantern room |
| 1857 | | Lewis | | Welch requested move |
| 1858 | Hughes | | | |
| 1861 | Wallace | | | |
| 1866 | | Gilpin | Joseph Bennett | Appointment of 3rd light-keeper |
| 1867 | Jeremiah Howgego | | | |
| 1868 | | Griffiths | | Gilpin moved as wife very ill |
| 1869 | | John J. Chavener | | Griffiths removed as unfitted to the service |
| 1871 | | | William J. Reece | |
| 1874 | Roberts | Brown | | Howgego, Chavener, Reece moved to other stations |
| 1876 | | | George Maskell | |
| 1879 | | | | Roberts moved to another station |
| 1879 | James Parsons | | | |
| 1880 | | Tom Whitchurch | | Brown moved to another station |
| 1882 | | | Wilson | Maskell dismissed for drinking |
| 1884 | John McCarthy | | | |
| 1886 | | Samuel Mayor Hast | | Whitchurch moved to another station. Locum arrived |
| 1887 | | | John Robert Hall | Wilson moved to another station |
| 1892 | | | | Superintendent April-May, keepers ill |
| 1893 | Trehair | | | McCarthy moved to another station |
| 1895 | | Gear | | Hast moved to another station |
| 1897 | | | | Trehair and 2 AKs moved to South Light |

# FOG SIGNAL STATION

| Year | Principal | Assistant | Notes |
|------|-----------|-----------|-------|
| 1862 | Thomas Lee | John Blackmore | Removed due to overcrowding and as Lee was unfit |
| 1873 | John Morgan | Thomas James | |
| 1874 | | David Nicholas | |
| 1876 | | Thomas James | James returned |
| 1889 | Nestor | | Locum August–September for Morgan, ill |
| 1890 | | Banner | James left once more |
| 1892 | Paul | | Mrs Morgan died, Morgan retired |
| 1894 | Savrall | | |
| 1897 | | | Banner moved to another station, not replaced as Battery to be closed down. |

# Appendix 2

## OWNERS, TENANTS AND LESSEES OF LUNDY

| Year | Owner | Tenant farmer | Lessee | Notes |
|------|-------|---------------|--------|-------|
| 1803 | Sir Vere Hunt | | | By purchase |
| 1818 | Sir Aubrey de Vere Hunt | | | Inherited |
| 1830 | John Matravers & Wm Stiffe | | | By purchase |
| 1836 | William Hudson Heaven | | | By purchase (resident after 1851) |
| 1839 | | Robert Rowles | | |
| 1847 | | John Lee | | Until 1860 (last of tenant farmers) |
| 1863 | | | William C. McKenna | For Lundy Granite Co. until 1871 |
| 1869 | | | Henry Benthall | Lessee until 1870 |
| 1883 | Rev Hudson Grosett Heaven | | | Son of William Hudson Heaven; held island in entail |
| 1885 | | | Thomas Wright | Lessee of entire island except Heaven reserve until 1891 |
| 1891 | | | Henry Ackland | Lessee of Stores (also farm in 1892) |
| 1894 | | | Thomas Dickinson | Joint lessee with Henry Ackland (until 1898) |
| 1897 | | | P. Napier Miles | Lease of Old Light until 1907 |
| 1899 | | | George Taylor | Sub-lessee William F. Saunt 1908–11 |
| 1916 | Walter Hudson Heaven | | | Nephew of the Revd Hudson Heaven |
| 1918 | Augustus Langham Christie | | | By purchase |
| 1920 | | | C. Herbert May | Sub-let Old Light to Plunket Greene family until 1925 |
| 1925 | Martin Coles Harman | | | By purchase |
| 1954 | Albion P. Harman | | | Held in trust. Joint owner with sisters Mrs Ruth Harman Jones and Mrs Diana Pennington Keast |
| 1969 | The National Trust | | The Landmark Trust | Purchased by gift of Sir Jack Hayward |

# Appendix 3

## WRECKS ON LUNDY 1610–1897

Of Lundy, Larn and Larn (1995) observe that

> "There are no very early accounts of wrecks here…presumably due to its isolation, lack of regular communication with the mainland, and the inherent benefit to the islanders of timber, coal, and other materials derived from wreck, which was best not reported to the authorities."

Wrecks listed below occurred either on Lundy or within the Lundy area. It should be noted that the various sources are not always in agreement in the classification of vessels.

| Year | Name of vessel | Notes |
|------|----------------|-------|
| 15–16th Century | (Not known) | protected marine archaeological site |
| 1610–20 | *Daniel* | |
| 19 Sep 1757 | *Marie* | collier |
| 4 Sep 1768 | *Susanna* | brigantine |
| 12 Jul 1792 | *Jane* | brigantine |
| Feb 1793 | *Nancy & Betty* | |
| 1793 | *Polly Bray* | |
| Dec 1796 | *Wye* | brig, lost with all crew |
| 20 Jan 1797 | *Jenny* | schooner |
| Feb 1797 | (Not known) | timber hoy captured by the French and scuttled |

Mr Gay is just arrived express from the Island of Lundy, and reports, that three French frigates and a lugger, anchored on the south side of the Island on Monday evening, and on Tuesday morning, took a timber hoy, in sight of the island, unbent her sails and scuttled her, and then stood up-Channel in sight of Ilfracombe and tacked and stood to Westward. Mr Gay boarded the timber hoy after she was scuttled, but the lugger standing towards them was obliged to quit her, and informed a brig of the fleet, who persisted in standing towards them; and was captured. *The African Queen*, from hence to Africa, passed Lundy at 12 o'clock at night.

The Times (1797)

| 14 Jan 1800 | *Myrtle Tree* | brigantine |
| 8 Feb 1809 | *Baltic* | |
| 20 Nov 1810 | *Concord* | |
| 1811 | *Estrella De Mar* | schooner |
| Dec 16 1811 | (Not known) | brigantine |
| 16 Nov 1816 | *Rover* | sloop |
| Feb 1819 | (Not known) | |
| 1 May 1819 | *Unity* | sloop |
| 20 Jan 1820 | *Lamb* | schooner |
| 7 Feb 1822 | *Fame* | cutter |
| 29 Oct 1823 | *Morreston* | brigantine |
| 14 Apr 1825 | *Commerce* | brigantine; all the crew survived |
| 25 Apr 1827 | *IO* | schooner |
| Nov 1828 | *La Jeune Emma* | |
| Dec 1828 | (Not known) | Russian squadron rescued by 2 pilots |
| 21 Mar 1829 | *Francis Anne* | brigantine |
| 28 April 1829 | *Hope* | brig |

### Clovelly, April 29

We lament the duty of announcing the loss, with all her crew, except the captain, of the *Hope* brig…on 27th ult, off Hartland Point. The disastrous particulars are detailed in the following letter from the captain to the owners:

Gentlemen, With a shaking hand and aching heart I send you very melancholy news. We came round land yesterday morning…with a fine breeze from the W to WNW. Between nine and ten it began to freshen, we shortened our canvas in proportion…a most ugly cross sea running, the vessel washed very much, still everything went very well. At half past four we made Lundy Island, and at five the wind began to cast more ahead; now we began to feel the effects of a heavy sea; we hove all the deals overboard from the lee side of the decks; I desired the men to draw the pump out, and then we would try if she would bear her foresail. Whilst they were so doing, a heavy sea struck her, and laid her on her beam ends: the boy Loveless, being to leeward, was washed away, and we saw no more of him. Scarce one minute elapsed before she was on her broadside, masts under water. The rest of us got out on her side, except the boy Trood, who was and still is in the cabin, clinging fast to the chainbolts. A skiff belonging to this place…hove about to come towards us; but something on board gave way, which detained her from rendering us assistance. We had been on her side about half an hour, with much anxiety watching the…skiff…At length she sank. We were now four of us fighting between life and death, nearly exhausted…each of us got hold of a deal, which we clung to…her stern rose up perpendicular, and down she went head foremost. Surls and Doddridge …I expect the suck of the vessel drew them down, as I never saw anything of them afterwards…At last, to my great joy, I saw the skiff approach…they soon came up, hove me a rope, which I caught hold of. I fell off the deals: they hauled me alongside, and got me on board, after being about an hour in the water. The mate was not far from me; they immediately tried for him and hove him the rope, which he caught, but being very weak he could not hold it in his hands; he put it in his mouth and they hauled him alongside when I suppose his mouth getting full of water, he sunk and was seen no more of, leaving me the only survivor of the crew. I experienced every attention on board the skiff…and am now here with only an old pair of trowsers and a shirt, all the clothes I have…

(The Times 1829)

| | | |
|---|---|---|
| 12 Jan 1833 | *Unity* | smack |
| 14 Mar 1833 | *Erin* | |
| 21 Aug 1835 | *Rapid* | collier; crew saved |
| Apr 1836 | *Abbotsford* | barque; damaged, leaking, returned to Bristol |
| 8 Oct 1836 | (Not known) | Danish ship with leak sunk to west of Lundy; 7 crew rescued from their drifting boat |
| 1838 | (Not known) | "belonging to Shields" |
| 1841 | *Sarah* | |
| Dec 1841 | *Mary* | run into by the *Odin* and put into Penarth, full of water |
| 1841 | *Eliza* | brigantine |
| 19 Mar 1842 | *Mariner* | smack |
| 25 Jun 1842 | *Crescent* | brigantine; crew saved |
| 2 Feb 1848 | *Ann* | schooner, in thick fog; one passenger survived |
| 12 Feb 1848 | *Sylphiden* | brigantine, in fog; crew hauled up the cliff by islanders with ropes. |
| 2 Feb 1849 | *Valiant* | brigantine |
| 7 Nov 1849 | *Archelaus* | |
| 2 Jan 1850 | (Not known) | barque |
| 18 Jan 1850 | *Thomas Crisp* | brigantine |
| 18 Feb 1850 | *Louisa* | sloop |
| 20 Feb 1850 | (Not known) | trawler (possibly *Medea*) |
| 29 May 1850 | *Glenlyon* | barque, towed off |
| 9 Jan 1851 | (Not known) | schooner |
| 9 Jan 1851 | (Not known) | French lugger |
| Sep 1851 | *Columbine* | back to Pill, leaking |
| 13 Jan 1852 | *Wizard* | schooner |
| 30 Apr 1853 | *Ariel* | brigantine |
| Nov 1853 | *Leocadie* | collision near Lundy; crew landed on island in ship's boat |
| 14 May 1855 | *Joseph F Votsam* | emigrant ship from Wales; passengers landed in ship's boats |
| 15 May 1855 | *Avon* | barque; sank immediately on striking, crew picked up in their boat and landed at Swansea |
| 1855 | | 7 marine casualties on or near Lundy |
| 18 Jan 1856 | *Wesleyana* | steamship |
| 11 Aug 1856 | *Loire* | steamship |
| 4 Nov 1857 | *Frederick* | smack; lost while at anchor, towed to Clovelly |
| 13 Mar 1858 | *Charles* | schooner |
| 9 Apr 1858 | *Trident* | smack |
| 1858 | | 15 vessels lost at Lundy |
| 25 Oct 1859 | (Not known) | 7 unidentified vessels lost in severe "Royal Charter Gale"; 4 seamen buried on Lundy; island "covered with wreck" |
| 1 Nov 1859 | *Diligent* | cutter |
| 16 Nov 1859 | *Peace* | smack |
| 9 Feb 1861 | *Lewis Charles* | schooner |
| 23 May 1861 | *Valentine* | brigantine, near lighthouse, in fog; ship lost, crew saved |
| 8 Oct 1861 | *Alert* | barque; leaking, sunk off Lundy; crew saved |

| | | |
|---|---|---|
| 11 Nov 1861 | *Ranger* | brigantine; sunk off Lundy after contact with *Éclair* |
| 16 Nov 1861 | (Not known) | wreckage washed up |
| 19 Mar 1862 | *James* | schooner; lost 15 miles E of Lundy; one survivor landed on Lundy; 4 sailors buried on the island (Chellew, Wallace, Matria and Garvey) |
| June 1862 | *Wesleyan* | schooner |
| 3 Nov 1862 | *Ben McCree* | |
| 2 Jan 1864 | *Iona II* | paddle steamer; wreck identified within the Marine Reserve, designated a protected site |
| 4 Apr 1864 | *Matilda* | steamship |
| 1 Oct 1864 | *Superior* | schooner |
| 28 Mar 1865 | *Hector* | steamship |
| 5 Apr 1865 | *Eclipse* | |
| 10 Jan 1866 | *Hannah More* | full-rigged sailing ship |
| 23 Mar 1866 | *Olive Branch* | schooner |
| 1866 | | 18 wrecks on Lundy |
| 7 Oct 1867 | *Alphonse* | |
| 27 Oct 1867 | *El Columba* | barque |
| 22 Dec 1867 | *West Dock* | wrecked on West Side, crew saved |
| 1867 | *Firefly* | |
| 1867 | | 16 wrecks on Lundy |
| Jan 1868 | *East Anglian* | steamship |
| 19 Feb 1868 | *Caroline* | smack; wrecked with a load of Lundy granite; six islanders roped the crew to the beach |
| 24 Apr 1868 | *Trelissick* | schooner |
| Aug 1868 | *The Admiral of Jersey* | barque; sank, one man rescued by pilot |
| Oct 1868 | *Swift* | schooner |
| 1 Nov 1868 | *Julia* | schooner |
| 7 Nov 1868 | *William* | smack |
| 1868 | | 16 casualties on Lundy |
| 30 Jan 1869 | *Herminia* | brigantine |
| 19 Mar 1869 | *Albion* | pilot cutter No. 9. dragged anchor in Lundy Roads; crew hauled to the beach by two fishermen. |
| 8 Apr 1869 | *Belinda* | brigantine, in fog; crew landed at Ilfracombe |
| 22 Apr 1869 | *Margaret* | brigantine |
| 30 Dec 1869 | *Eliza* | smack |
| March 1870 | *Crystal Palace* | struck on Lundy; put into Milford, sinking |
| 21 May 1870 | *Asterias* | barque; blown up by ignition of coal gas; capt and one seaman killed; two boats landed twelve crew at Penzance |
| 24 Oct 1870 | *Thomas Varcoe* | schooner |
| 16 Dec 1870 | *Mary* | brigantine; subsequent enquiry deprived the master of his certificate for three months for taking an unnecessary risk |
| 1870 | *John Brogden* | |
| 14 Feb 1871 | *Brenda* | full-rigged sailing ship; towed off later |
| 3 April 1871 | *Cornwall* | collided with *Himalaya* in fog |
| 5 Feb 1872 | *Mary* | fore-and-after; crew saved |
| 5 Apr 1872 | *New House* | |

| | | |
|---|---|---|
| 7 May 1872 | *Gertrude* | brigantine |
| 8 May 1872 | *Ostrich* | sank in the Roads after a collision; crew saved |
| 10 Nov 1872 | (Not known) | schooner dismasted |
| 1872 | | 9 casualties at Lundy |
| 27 Mar 1873 | *Eliza* | brigantine |
| 26 Oct 1873 | Pilot skiff No 37 | collision with skiff No 4, which rescued the crew |
| 1873 | | 10 casualties at Lundy |
| Jan 1874 | *Fingal* | steamship |
| 7 June 1874 | *Providence* | smack |
| 7 June 1874 | Pilot skiff No 19 | |
| 30 Sep 1874 | *Fanny* | smack |
| 1875 | | 8 wrecks at Lundy |
| 1 Jan 1876 | *Jean et Robert* | schooner |
| 1876 | | 12 wrecks at Lundy |
| 7 Feb 1877 | *Ethel* | steamship, one survivor |
| 29 Oct 1880 | (Not known) | |
| 17 Nov 1880 | Pilot Boat No 5 | two crew washed overboard and drowned |
| 9 Dec 1880 | *Rattler* | trawler; collision with *Amazon* |
| Oct 1881 | (Not known) | |
| 20 Dec 1881 | *Marco Polo* | brigantine; capsized, crew saved |
| 26 Nov 1881 | *Cambronne* | (or possibly *Cambrian*) steamship; collision with *Marion* |
| 31 Aug 1882 | *Il Paola Ravello* | barque; pulled off by tugs |
| 13 Dec 1882 | *Burnswark* | barque; towed off |
| 13 Dec 1882 | *Heroine* | barquentine; ashore, crew landed at Cardiff |
| Dec 1882 | *Albrecht* | brigantine; leaking, got off and towed to Penarth |
| Feb 1883 | (Not known) | barque |
| Feb 1883 | (Not known) | steamer |
| 23 Sep 1883 | *Little Ruth* | on fire, got off later |
| 27 Jan 1884 | *Hornet* | steamship; sank after leak; crew lost except one boy |
| 27 Jun 1884 | *Wimbledon* | steamship; leaking |
| 27 Jun 1884 | *Baines Hawkins* | steamship |
| 27 Jul 1884 | (Not known) | steamer |
| Oct 1884 | *Roebuck* | steamer; refloated and returned to Cardiff |
| 21 Dec 1884 | *William Banks* | steamer; collision in Lundy Roads with *Vagliano Brothers*; severe damage, returned to Cardiff |
| 11 Feb 1885 | *Peer of the Realm* | steamship; struck in fog and half full of water; crew saved |
| 20 Apr 1885 | (Not known) | schooner damaged on rocks in fog; got off later |
| 15 Oct 1886 | *Bosweden* | schooner; wreckage washed ashore (gale) |
| 16 Oct 1886 | *Inversnaid* | full-rigged sailing ship; crew lost (gale) |
| 17 Oct 1886 | *Juanita* | gale |
| 30 Jan 1888 | *Elsie* | steamship; got off, went to Cardiff |
| 6 Feb 1888 | *Zaire* | steamship |
| 14 Feb 1888 | *New Prosperous* | pilot cutter No 3; all hands saved |
| Mar 1888 | *City of Exeter* | |
| 9 May 1888 | *Radnor* | steam tug; crew landed on the island; refloated |
| 9 May 1888 | (Not known) | burning vessel (? Boucan) |

| | | |
|---|---|---|
| 9 May 1888 | *Electric* | tug |
| 16 Dec 1889 | *Eliza Jones* | schooner |
| Mar 1890 | *Benamain* | floated off, but sank off the Mumbles; crew landed at Swansea by a pilot boat |
| 10 Sept 1890 | *Ashdale* | steamship |
| Mar 1891 | *Gladiolus* | ran ashore and damaged, put back to Cardiff |
| 20 Nov 1891 | *Tasfield* | steamship |
| 1891 | *Bygda* | |
| 19 Feb 1892 | *Tunisie* | steamship |

The steamer *Tunisie*…which left Cardiff on Thursday with coal for Marseilles, went ashore on Friday morning on Lundy island, and remained fast on the rocks under a high cliff. There are no life-saving appliances on the island, but the inhabitants fixed a line to a signal rocket and, after three attempts, succeeded in throwing a line over the ship. The crew were thus got on shore one by one and hauled up the cliff in a bag. There is no telegraphic communication with the island, and it was not until Sunday night that a tug arrived in reply to the signals and conveyed a message to Cardiff requesting assistance. The steamer is full of water, and fast by the stern on the rocks.

(The Times 1892)

| | | |
|---|---|---|
| 20 Apr 1892 | *Ackworth* | steamer, in fog; crew saved |
| Nov 1892 | (Not known) | tug |
| 13 Aug 1893 | *Charles W Anderson* | steamship |
| 21 Nov 1893 | *Favourite* | |
| 1 Dec 1893 | *Ismyr* | brigantine; at Rat Island; total loss, two men lost |
| 14 May 1895 | *Coila* | brigantine |
| 19 Sep 1895 | *Maria* | steamship; crew saved |
| 10 Nov 1895 | (Not known) | ship under tow |
| 23 May 1896 | *Kate* | schooner |
| 19 Sept 1896 | *Maria* | steamship near Quarry quay |
| 10 Oct 1896 | *Sastie* | brigantine |
| Jan 1897 | *Mystery* | pilot cutter; crew saved by the tug, *Red Rose* |
| 22 Jan 1897 | *Dyfed* | pilot cutter |
| 18 Mar 1897 | *Cam* | steamship; put back to Barry |
| 21 Mar 1897 | *Salado* | steamship |
| Mar 1897 | *Telephone* | smack; lost her anchors in the Roads |
| Mar 1897 | *Diamond* | smack; crew saved |
| 1 Apr 1897 | *Millicent* | ketch |
| 19 May 1897 | *Infanta* | ketch |
| 19 May 1897 | *Yeo* | |
| 21 Aug 1897 | *Grimsby* | |
| 31 Aug 1897 | *Rover* | lighter |
| 2 Nov 1897 | *Ballydoon* | steamship |

# Appendix 4

## LIGHTHOUSE ORDER BOOK: EXTRACTS

Visits by Trinity House personnel 1854–97
AIEO: All in excellent order; AIGO: All in good order; AIO: All in order

1858 6 Aug Captain Close accompanied by Mr Burgess on the subject of the Lightning conductor. AIGO.

1859 8 Aug Captains Pixley, Were, Bayley, Arrow. AIGO. Recently painted in satisfactory manner. Estimates to be considered.

1860 21 May Captains Close, Nisbet. AIGO. Recommend estimate for new ranges to be accepted as the present ones are worn out. Committee have ordered the assistant keepers' copper in the Out House to be placed in accordance with Mr Slee's estimate which includes iron work and wooden covers i.e. £1.12.3. Cesspools to be emptied & Roof of Dwellings for which an estimate is to be obtained and sent up, also the rain water cisterns.

1861 18 June Captains Redman, Shuttleworth, Arrow, visited the establishment and delivered annual stores. Keepers to finish painting interior, Gates, Flagstaff and to whitewash outhouses and cellars. Estimate for whitewashing Boundary and garden walls. Stones on road approved £6.6.0 and ordered to proceed. £0.10.0 new hinges and sash lines approved to proceed. Keepers to procure lime from the [fog station] works for Gun Station and to get the Boundary Stones hardened up when the workmen are about by Mr Douglass' men. Keeper to get a short piece of Tubing made to form continuous chimney in lantern and to increase overflow.

21 June Same Committee visited at Midnight and found a very good solid flame of 2 inches and everything in excellent order, the continuous chimney has been fitted very expeditiously and improved the light much. The Lantern Door is obliged to be often open as there is no ventilation else whatever externally. Nothing save the draught up the tower. No cylinders have been sent with the Stores.

1862 23 Apr Captain Nelly. The place was not in such good order as he could have wished. Order Mr Douglass men to put new Braids under the oil lanterns when pouring oil in them. 21 July Captain Were with Mr Douglass to inspect the Gun House, which has been injured by Firing – found 3 men at work from Penzance left here by Mr James Douglass last Wednesday.

Some small supplies required for the Gun establishment: White lead and boiled oil; Printed instructions for Gunmen; A Hand-spike - Barometer and Thermometer; An Order Book and box of library ditto; Bell for each cottage; Medicine Chest - Tin Letter Box; More oil tins for about 100 galls and a lengthened Pipe mouth to start from outside window of Tower.

1864 17 June Captains Nisbet, Weller, Lambert with annual supplies - an S hook to be made and 2 weights of 7lb each to add to the weight of the revolving machinery when necessary. Front doors to be grained and painted by painters.

15 Aug Captain Nisbet. Wilkins mechanic at work on Revolving Machine. More attention to be paid to the cleanliness of the Dioptric Lamp. Mr Wallace's dwelling to be cleaned out at once ready for the new Principal, and the expenses incurred to be sent by the Agent and charged against Mr Wallace.

1865 19 July Captain Were, Mr Evans accompanied. AIGO. Sanctioned necessary estimates. Mr Evans, the Superintendent, to get an estimate for enclosing the lower part of Corporation's land, by stone, and also by a stout wire fence.

1866 15 May Captain Nisbet. Mr Tabb and his people here carrying out the usual course of painting throughout, all the small necessary repairs to be carried out at once, so that the painters may not be delayed.

21 June Captains Weller, Lambert with annual supplies - found the revolving apparatus working too quickly by 20" to each face - ordered the principal to have it corrected immediately... all the painting just completed.

1867 12 Aug Captains Shuttleworth, Fenwick with supplies. AIGO, but more care should be taken in cutting the wicks of the lamp even.

1868 28 July Captains Close, Lambert, annual supply in Argus. The contract to be obtained from the Granite Co. for limewashing Boundary walls, outhouses, etc. as hitherto.

1869 28 July Captains Webb, Rodman, Shuttleworth. IVGO. Committee enquired into reported misconduct of AK Griffiths and Superintendent is directed to obtain medical certificate of his state of health and forward same to the House.

1870 13 Aug Captains Nisbet, Bayly, Lambert in Argus with annual supplies. AIO. Mr Tabb and men painting the establishment. Mr Howgego, PK, has 10 days leave to go to the mainland for medical advice.

1874 24 Aug Captains Nisbet, Lambert, Atkins in Vestal. Mr Tabb and gang painting establishment. New piece of oilcloth to be procured for floor inside of lens. New floor for PK Woodhouse [also small repairs specified]. Gun Station: Guns and magazine IGO. Cocoanut matting to be procured for the floors of two rooms. Pipe leading from Tank to Water Closet to be repaired. PK J Howgego has leave for one week early in September to visit mainland for medical advice.

1875 3 Aug Captains Fenwick, Shuttleworth, Were. Refer to visiting book at Gun Station for requirements there. David Nicholas to have 14 days leave.

1876 15 July Captains Atkins, Bayly, Lambert by Argus with supplies. Found the whole of the establishment, with exception of the Assistant (George Maskell) dwelling, in a very neglected and unsatisfactory condition. The keepers have not been able to obtain lime on the island. Mr Evans will be instructed to send a sufficient supply immediately.

1878 17 July Captains Webb, Ladds, in Siren (first trip) with annual supplies together with the new fog signal Cotton Powder Rockets to be substituted for the Gun on 1st August. The keys of the Store where rockets are stored to be kept in PK's room to be demanded of him by Principal Gunner when required. No lights or smoking in the vicinity to be permitted. Establishment under course of painting.

1879 13 Aug Captains Nisbet, Shuttleworth in Siren. John Morgan, Gunner, has permission to go the mainland for a week to get medical advice as soon as Alfred Brown, AK, returns from his present absence.

1880 13 May Captain Burne by Siren. Captain Bayly too unwell to land. Attention of the PK called to the careful timing of the revolutions of the lens by frequent observation when working.

4 Sept Mr Evans, Superintendent. AIGO. Lamps leaking, mechanic to be sent for.

1881 2 June Mr Evans. New lamp working well.

23 Aug Captains Were, Atkins, Bayly, Lambert by Argus. Mr Evans to supply a spirit level for the adjustment of the burner. Bedroom chairs, washstand and 2 Windsor chairs required.

27 Sept Captain Burne by Siren, on special service. Superintendent to enquire respecting drawers for Whitchurch's dwelling, for which dimensions have been taken for some time since.

1882 19 May William Lile, Superintendent. The drawers for Whitchurch not allowed – a spirit level supplied.

28 Aug Galatea with supply of rockets and explosives. Painters at work.

11 Sept Superintendent Lile visited and inspected Lights burning, good flame high light 31/2 inches, the Asgard lamps burning fairly well.

1883 1 Feb Superintendent Lile. Low light reflectors rather dull and paintwork black, said to be caused by smoke of lamps, the tubes being out of order.

15 May I have to signify the directions of the EB that the signal DNS 'Is there anything to prevent landing' shall in future be understood to mean 'Is it safe to land?' the keepers answering the signal by the affirmative or negative pennant.

9 June Superintendent. Limewashing finished, water tanks cleared out – water very good.

1884 4 Feb Superintendent accompanied Mr Ayers to examine the lightning conductor re the Tower having been struck by lightning on 26th ult damaging speaking pipes and door leading into tower and breaking 15 panes of glass in tower windows. Mason and carpenter now on island to be employed to make good damage and roofs of cottages.

1884 18 June Superintendent. Water tanks to be cleaned out.

23 Sept Captains Ladds, Atkins. Keepers at lighthouse to fire rockets when there is fog to the Eastward of the island and at night at the lighthouse, until the fog signal men take it up, and one dozen to be kept in the oil store cupboard for the purpose until further orders from the House. When any of the keepers is sick or unfit for duty one of the Gunners (when not required for rocket duty) is to assist at the lighthouse as PK may direct.

1885 10 Mar One of the AKs to take first watch at Fog Station and to assist as required during the absence of Morgan now going to Cardiff as witness on a trial.

24 Jul Whitchurch AK on watch.

1886 4 Aug Establishment now undergoing 4th yearly painting throughout.

1887 27 May Annual painting nearly finished.

1889 2 Aug Captains Vyvyan, Weller in Siren. Mr Morgan ill and one of AKs to take his work alternately...to report on facilities for saving water as PK reports unnecessary waste. New period of revolution is accurate and lenses an improvement.

1890 12 May Mason now on island to open out drain of PK dwelling - smells badly in the house.

11 Sept Sir Sidney Webb, Captain Ladds, Rt. Hon. The President of the Board of Trade, Sir Michael E. Hicks Beach.

1892 21 Apr Superintendent visited with Mr Matthews to arrange about extension of landing slip at the beach.

11 May Captains Barlow, Stewart for the purpose of presenting the testimonial presented by the R.N.L.I. to Mr McCarthy for his gallant successful exertions in rescuing the crew of 21 persons from the wreck of the French steamer Tunisie on February 19th 1892, a donation of 15 shillings each was at the same time granted to 10 others who were associated with him on that occasion. John McCarthy PK, S M Hast AK, J Hall 2nd AK, John Lee Labourer, Mr Ackland Grocer [lessee], Samuel Randle Labourer, James Dunn Labourer, William Richards Mason, Christopher Ward Gardener, George Thomas Fisherman, John Jewell Blacksmith

19 Aug Nothing seems to have been done about the water since the visit 3 years ago. Superintendent to remind the House about it.

20 Aug Royal Commission on Electrical Communication of Lighthouses the Earl of Mountedgecombe, Sir Ed. Birkbeck, Admiral Sir F. McClintlock, Vice Admiral Sir George Neres, J. Cannon Lamb, H. L. Mulholland M.P., B. Munro Ferguson, M.P., G. Graves, Garham Roper Sec. Necessary information obtained from PK and Hall.

1894 29 Jan PK Trehair in charge since 27.11.1893.

26 Jul Mr Ackland's tender of £3.3.0. approved.

1897 1 Feb Duty at Fog Station by AKs alternating Gunner Paul having been sent to Flamborough Head.

28 Aug Inventory of furniture etc for transfer to new lighthouse.

2 Nov Arranged transfer of stores.

11 Nov Arranged transfer of staff to new lighthouses.

19 Nov [The new lighthouses were brought into use].

15 Dec Permanent lantern and lamp in use, keepers gradually getting familiar with new lamp and 5 inch burner.

# Appendix 5

## MATERIALS FROM WHICH THE BUILDING AND FINISHINGS ARE CONSTRUCTED

GROUND FLOOR FIRST STAGE The foundation of tower consists of ten courses of brick, spreading 8 inches on each side of the wall line, the floor is paved with purbec stone: brick nogged partitions plastered, the ceiling is lathed and plastered. The walls limewhited, the entrance door of 2 inch deal in six panels and framed square, the other doors are proper ledged hung with cross garnetts [T-shaped hinges] with rebated door frames, deal cased frame oak sunk sill and Inch ½ ovolo sashes fixed to Oil Store window, in this opening an extra sash is fixed to form a double casement.

STAIRCASE is of Inch ¼ deal treads, risers and carriages, the soffits lined with ¾ beaded lining, rounded rail and square newells. Deal cased frames oak sunk sills and Inch ½ ovolo sashes, single hung with lines and weights the windows on Landings Inch ½ rounded window boards, the linings plastered.

SECOND STAGE The floor consists of Inch ./4 deal on joists 9 x 3 the ends of which lie on a circular plate 6 x 4, in the centre of the tower runs a beam 12 x 9 whose ends lie on two templates and support the joists, the room is skirted with inch square skirting, the partitions are bricknogged and plastered, the ceiling lathed and plastered, a fire place in this room with portland hearth, with mantle and jambs, wood moulding round same with a deal shelf supported on brackets above, the doors are beaded and ledged hung on cross garnetts and the openings lined with rebated linings, the window frames and sashes same as described on Staircase.

THIRD STAGE CONTAINING THE LOW LIGHT The floor joists plate and girder same as described to Second Stage, the Lamp Room floor is cased with copper, the rooms are skirted with deal square skirting, the sash and frame in Bed Room as before described on Staircase. The Lamp Room window is of iron containing nine squares of plate glass with an iron casement in centre pane, an Inch ½ deal rounded window board, the linings plastered. For a description of the Lamps and their Reflectors vide drawing No 7, the doors are beaded and ledged on cross garnetts, Inch ¼ single rebated linings.

FOURTH STAGE The finishing and materials the same as in the Second Stage, an iron pipe runs through this Story to convey the smoke of the Low Light lamps into the upper Lamp Stage from whence it discharges itself through the roof of said upper stage.

UPPER LAMP STAGE The floor is of Inch deal lined with copper on joists 9 x 3 ends of which lie on a circular plate 6 x 4, the centre of same on a beam 12 x 9, the external Gallery is supported on 32 blocks projecting within 3 Inches of the edge and 12½ x 6, running through wall as shewn in Section which rests the plate of the polygon which is 8 x 4 in which framed the posts 5½ x 4 with crossbraces 4 x 2; five sides of polygon are lined externally with inch luffer boards and internally with inch beaded boarding, another side is occupied with an Inch ¼ ledged and beaded door, hung on cross garnetts and two rough rebated stops on posts to form jamb linings, the remaining ten are filled in with an iron frame 1⅛ x ⅝ rivetted together with cross pieces at angles as shown in Section, 7½ sides of the polygon which is fitted with iron work is glazed with plate glass, the remaining 2½ sides with knotted glass now painted over, the iron frame is fixed on a sill of wood 5 x 4¼ which is covered with lead and has a small lead trough at the internal edge for the conveying of the water that may beat through the sashes; the upper curb of polygon for the reception of the rafters feet of roof where iron frame exists is of iron Inch x 3" the remaining sides of wood 8½ x 4, on which are fixed the rafters they are 2¼ x ⅝ in thickness and have two iron stays between each 1¾ x ¼ with ends turned up and rivetted through each other, the curb of roof is of iron one foot in diameter and 6 inches in depth ¾ thick, through which the ends of the rafters are inserted and pinned; the cowl is of copper with an iron standard through the centre, the roof is covered with copper and has four appertures in same, in which are fitted four fluted cowls for the escape of the smoke from the lamps. The enclosure to stairs is formed of posts 4 x 3 on which is nailed inch boarding, a ledged door on cross garnetts at head of

Stairs. The Lamp and its Reflector described in drawing No 7 the Gallery is lined with lead and has a gutter sunk in same for the conveyance of the rain water into tanks, it has an iron railing round same consisting of standards 5 feet 3" apart and 1¼ square moulded top rail 1" x 2"¼ bottom rail 1" x 1⅛ fitted in with inch square bars, 1¼ beaded boarding across the gallery as shown in drawing No 4.

The external surface of the Tower is compoed and painted red, the dressings to windows as shewn in drawing No 5, the copper pipe shewn in this drawing projecting over the right hand window, third Stage is for the conveyance of the smoke from the Stove of Low Light.

THE LIVING ROOM is paved with purbec and skirted with inch deal square skirting, the ceiling lathed and plastered partly to rafters, the walls plastered and colored, the windows consist of deal cased frames, oak sunk sills, the sash looking SSW is made to slide the other is fixed. Inch ¼ square framed shutters to the window, and inch rounded window boards, stone mantle and jambs to fireplace and deal shelf over, one of the recesses next chimney breast is fitted up with an Oven, the other with a deal dwarf cupboard with shelves over; the door is beaded and ledged, hung with cross Garnetts and rebated linings in opening, stone sink as in drawing No 2

WASH HOUSE is paved with purbec, the walls limewhited, ceiling partly lathed and plastered, door beaded and ledged and a deal sash and frame to window. The Privy ceiling is lathed and plastered, the walls render set and colored, deal seat, riser and bearers, deal floor and joists, beaded and ledged door hung on cross garnetts. The fronts of Living Room, Wash-house and Privy are covered with composition and painted red, the former building is slated, the ridge covered with lead, the two latter roofs are covered with plain tiles, there are two water tanks in Yard consisting of inch ½ deal lined with lead for the reception of the rain water.

(Trinity House Engineer's Archive No. 818, 1819)

# REFERENCES

Allington, P., Greenhill, P., Youings, J. and Kennerly, A. (1994) Ship Handling and Hazards on the Devon Coast. M. Duffy, S. Fisher, B. Greenhill, D. Starkey and J Youngs (eds.) *The New Maritime History of Devon*, ii, University of Exeter.

Anon (*c.*1860) *North Devon Sketches*. Typescript, M. Ternstrom collection.

Ashley, Rvd J (1841–43) Diary. The Mission to Seafarers, London.

Bideford Gazette (1884) 29 July 1884.

Crespi, A. J. H. (1881) *Lundy Island*. The Temperance Record, 27 January.

Denham, Lt H. M. (1832) *Remarks & Sailing Directions Relative to Lundy Island*. J & J Mawdsley, Liverpool.

Dixon, C. (1973) *Henry Moffat, Seaman*. The Mariner's Mirror, lix, pg. 197.

Exeter Flying Post (1833) March 1833.

Exeter Flying Post (1842) 7 July 1842.

Hague, D. and Christie, R. (1975) *Lighthouses: Their Architecture, History and Archaeology*. pgs 109, 215. Gomer Press, Llandysul, Wales.

Findlay, A. G. (1861) *Lighthouses of the World*. pg 26. R. H. Laurie, London.

Findlay, A. G. (1885) *Lighthouses of the World*. 36th edition including *A List & Description of Coast Fog Signals*, 1880 by E. Price Edwards. R. H. Laurie, London.

Gade, F. W. (1978) *My Life on Lundy*. Privately published.

Gosse, P. (1853) *Lundy Island: The Home Friend* iii (57), pp 126–28.

Heaven Archive (1836) Family letters, 8 October 1836.

Heaven Archive (1884) Heaven family diary, 26–28 January 1884.

Heaven Archive (1885) Heaven family diary, February 12–April 16 1885.

Heaven Archive (1906) Catalogue of Sale.

Ilfracombe Chronicle (1873) 1 Nov 1873.

Illustrated Lundy News (1973) Issue No. 12.

Langham, A. (1994) *The Island of Lundy*. pg. 142. Alan Sutton, Stroud.

Larn, R. and Larn, B. (1995) *Shipwreck Index of the British Isles*, 1. Lloyd's Register of Shipping, London.

Le Messurier, B. (1992) *Life on Lundy 100 years ago*. North Devon Heritage, No.4, Appledore Maritime Museum.

Limerick Archive (1821–27) Correspondence to Sir Aubrey de Vere Hunt, T22. Ireland.

Lundy Field Society Archive (1946) Invitation to membership. http://www.lundy.org.uk

Lysons, Revd D. and Lysons S. (1822) *Magna Britannia*, vol vi, pg 580–581. Thomas Cadell, London.

Messurier, B. (1964) *Keeper of the Old Light*. Western Morning News, 21 September.

National Archives (1783) HMS *Beaver*. ADM 1/2 307 XC 32991.

National Archives (1829) Parliamentary Report. Microfiches 1829, 31.130–131.

National Archives (1834) Parliamentary Reports. Microfiches 1834, 37.79–85.

National Archives (1845) Parliamentary Reports. Microfiches 1845, 49.51–59.

National Archives (1861) Parliamentary Reports. Microfiches 1861, 67.216–231.

North Devon Journal (1866) 25 January 1866.

North Devon Journal (1883) 5 January 1883.

North Devon Journal (1868) 26 September 1868.

North Devon Record Office (1787) *Journal of the time I spent on the island of Lundy*. 3704/M/SS/LU/1.

Perry, R. (1940) *Lundy, Isle of Puffins*. pg. 18–19. Lindsay Drummond, London.

Smith, G. (1989) *Smuggling in the Bristol Channel, 1700-1850*. Countryside Books, Newbury.

Taunton Courier (1820) *Navigation of the Bristol Channel*. 6 January 1820.

The Times (1797) 9 February 1797.

The Times (1797) 25 February 1797.

The Times (1823) 12 November 1823.

The Times (1829) *Clovelly, April 29*. 8 May 1829.

The Times (1828) 23 December 1828.

The Times (1864a) 2 January 1864.

The Times (1864b) 8 April 1864.

The Times (1866) 5 March 1866.

The Times (1877) 9 February 1877.

The Times (1892) 23 February 1892.

The Times (1897) 19 November 1897.

Trinity House Engineer's Archive (1819) Isle of Wight, No. 818.

Trinity House Guildhall Library Archive (1812) 30152 *A Nautical Description of the Coast of Britain* iv, pg 67.

Trinity House Guildhall Library Archive (1751) 30004 Benson's petition xi, p. 126.

Trinity House Guildhall Library Archive (1803) 30010 Reply to Sir Vere Hunt xx, pg. 447.

Trinity House Guildhall Library Archive (1819) 30004 xvii, pg. 114.

Trinity House Guildhall Library Archive (1820) 30031 Description of the Light ix, pg. 99.

Trinity House Guildhall Library Archive (1819–20) 30031 Ledgers viii, pg. 577; ix pgs 55, 87, 125.

Trinity House Guildhall Library Archive (1824) 30010 Letter from Lt Crosbie xxiv, pg. 434.

Trinity House Guildhall Library Archive (1829) 30052 ii, pg. 37.

Trinity House Guildhall Library Archive (1830) 30010 xxxii, pg. 530; xxxiii, pg. 57, 72, 193. 221.

Trinity House Guildhall Library Archive (1831a) 30010 xxvii, pg. 449.

Trinity House Guildhall Library Archive (1831b) 30010 Letter from Mr Stiffe xxvii, pg. 547.

Trinity House Guildhall Library Archive (1834), 30052 iv, pg. 36.

Trinity House Guildhall Library Archive (1839a), 30025 xiii, pg. 2.

Trinity House Guildhall Library Archive (1839b) 30010 Death of Grant xxxi, pg. 368.

Trinity House Guildhall Library Archive (1839c) 30025 Agency transfer to Milford, xiii, pg. 11.

Trinity House Guildhall Library Archive (1839d) 30052 v, pg. 226.

Trinity House Guildhall Library Archive (1839 40) 30052 v, p.265.

Trinity House Guildhall Library Archive (1840a) 30025 xiii, pg. 363.

Trinity House Guildhall Library Archive (1840b) 30025 xiv, pgs 24, 85.

Trinity House Guildhall Library Archive (1841) 30004 xxii, pg. 154.

Trinity House Guildhall Library Archive (1842a) 30010 xxxiii, pg. 57.

Trinity House Guildhall Library Archive (1842b) 30010 New apparatus installed xxiii, pg. 328.

Trinity House Guildhall Library Archive (1844) 30004 xxiii, pg. 39.

Trinity House Guildhall Library Archive (1845) 30052 vi, pgs 119, 151.

Trinity House Guildhall Library Archive (1846) 30052 vi , pg. 151.

Trinity House Guildhall Library Archive (1857a) 30052 vii, pg. 463

Trinity House Guildhall Library Archive (1857b) 30052 vii, pgs 464, 488.

Trinity House Guildhall Library Archive (1857c) 30052 vii, pg. 432.

Trinity House Guildhall Library Archive (1858a) 30010 Letter from W. H. Heaven xli, pg. 360.

Trinity House Guildhall Library Archive (1858b) 30052 viii, pg. 44.

Trinity House Guildhall Library Archive (1858c) 30052 viii, pgs 13–16.

Trinity House Guildhall Library Archive (1862a) 30025 xxix, pgs 26, 40, 332.

Trinity House Guildhall Library Archive (1862b) 30052 viii, pg. 381.

Trinity House Guildhall Library Archive (1868a) 30010 xlvi, pgs 487, 550, 584; 30025 xxxvi pg. 52.

Trinity House Guildhall Library Archive (1868b) 30052 xi, pg. 230.

Trinity House Guildhall Library Archive (1868–71) 30004 xxix, pg. 316; 30010 xlvii, pg. 14; 30010 xlviii, pg. 251.

Trinity House Guildhall Library Archive (1871) 30010 xlvii, pg. 588; 30052 xi, pg. 435; 30010 xlvii, pgs 268, 292.

Trinity House Guildhall Library Archive (1873) 30052 xii, pg. 47; 30025 xi, pg. 207.

Trinity House Guildhall Library Archive (1874) 30025 xli, pg. 226.

Western Flying Post (1804) 2 July 1804.

# FURTHER READING

Bathurst, B. (1999) *The Lighthouse Stevensons*, Harper Collins, London.

Bouquet, M. (1963) *The Wreck of the Hannah More*. Sea Breezes, London.

Bouquet, M. (1967) Lundy Shipwrecks. *Lundy Field Society Annual Report*, No 18, pgs 19–23

Bouquet, M. (1969) More Lundy Shipwrecks. *Lundy Field Society Annual Report*, 20, pg. 22.

Britton, J. (1803) *The Beauties of England & Wales* 4. Vernor & Hood, London.

Devon Record Office (1819) Lundy Lighthouse: Report on Petition, 1819. QS 1/36 No 4125, Exeter.

*Encyclopaedia Britannica* (1946) vol 14, pgs 90–95, Chicago.

Fenwick, V. and Gale, A. (1998) *Historic Shipwrecks*. Tempus, Stroud

Heyes, M. J. (1994) A Preliminary Survey of the Wrecks within the Lundy Marine Nature Reserve. *Lundy Field Society Annual Report*, 45, pgs 77–85.

Jackson, D. (1975) *Lighthouses of England & Wales*. David & Charles, Newton Abbot.

Larn, R. (1974) *Devon Shipwrecks*. David & Charles, Newton Abbot.

Larn, R. (1996) *Shipwrecks of the Devon Coast*. Countryside Books, Newbury.

Minchinton, W. E. (1954) Bristol: Metropolis of the West in the Eighteenth Century. *Transactions of the Royal Historical Society*, 5th Series, vol 4.

Page, J. L. W. (1895) *The Coasts of Devon & Lundy Island*. Horace & Cox, London.

Robertson, P. C. (1994) *Marine Archaeology & Lundy Marine Nature Reserve*. Lundy Field Society Annual Report, 45, pgs 57–76.

Smith, G. (1980) *Something to Declare*. Harrap, London.

Sutton-Jones, K. (1985) *The Lighthouse Yesterday, Today & Tomorrow*. Michael Russell, Salisbury.

Ternstrom, M. (1996) Lundy from beach to Plateau: a reassessment. *Lundy Field Society Annual Report*, 47, pgs 77–86.

Ternstrom, M. (1998) Some Additions to the Lundy Wrecks List. *Lundy Field Society Annual Report*, 49, pgs 58–67.

Ternstrom, M. (1999) Lundy: An analysis and comparative study of the factors affecting the development of the island from 1577 to 1969. Unpublished PhD thesis (2 vols), Cheltenham & Gloucester College of Higher Education.

Thomas, S. (1959) *The Nightingale Scandal*, privately printed, Bideford. Reprinted 2001.

Woodman, R. and Wilson, J. (2002) *The Lighthouses of Trinity House*. Thomas Reed, Bradford on Avon.

Information about Lundy Field Society publications can be found at: http://www.lundy.org.uk